"Don't wait for your competition or a new entrant to renew your industry for you. This is a must read to help you read and use the turbulence around you to create the organizational capacity to continually renew."
—James C. Rush
Senior Vice President
Corporate Services
Bank of Montreal

"If you are information-overloaded in a turbulent environment—and who isn't—you should read this book. Stan Gryskiewicz's lively treatment of managing the meaning from constant input is both practical and stimulating."
—Dr. Lance Lindon
Managing Consultant, PA Consulting Group

"'Turbulence' is whatever you can't control or plan; how to make it 'positive'? From long experience helping companies enhance their creativity, Stan Gryskiewicz has developed an upbeat idea: stir the turbulence around you into your organization, as an agent of self-renewal and constructive change."
—Harlan Cleveland
President
World Academy of Art and Science

"Stan Gryskiewicz has brought positive turbulence into two of the organizations I have been leading. He has thorough knowledge and extensive experience in this area and knows what he is talking about."
—Ingar Skaug
President and CEO
Wilhelmsen Lines

"I can testify that these ideas can be put to use. We had some problems that were specific to our situation, but I experimented with many of the Positive Turbulence events Stan Gryskiewicz mentions, with good results."
—Bruce Wright
Director, Innovation (retired)
Hoechst Celanese Corp.

"This is not a book for every manager. It isn't a quick fix, but for those executives and entrepreneurs who are looking to build vibrant, creative organizations, that can give and take turbulence, this is a must read."

—J. David Placek, President

Lexicon Branding Incorporated

"Change can breathe new life or produce death within an organization. Constructively stimulating it through Positive Turbulence is one of the hidden keys to fostering innovation and creativity. By making clear something that has been invisible, Stan's unique approach is a major contribution to today's business leaders."

—Robert B. Rosenfeld

President & CEO

Idea Connections, a management consulting firm specializing in innovation

"Experiences contained within this book provide ideas for creativity and renewal that cross cultural borders."

—Yoshio Tomisaka

Vice Chairman

Japan Management Association

Center for
Creative Leadership
leadership. learning. life.

ABOUT THE CENTER FOR CREATIVE LEADERSHIP

The Center for Creative Leadership is an international, nonprofit, educational institution whose mission is to advance the understanding, practice, and development of leadership for the benefit of society worldwide. Founded in Greensboro, North Carolina, in 1970 by the Smith Richardson Foundation Inc., the Center is today one of the largest institutions in the world focusing on leadership. In addition to locations in Greensboro; Colorado Springs, Colorado; San Diego, California; and Brussels, Belgium, CCL has an office in New York City and maintains relationships with more than twenty-eight network associates and partners in the United States and abroad.

CCL conducts research, produces publications, and provides a variety of educational programs and products to leaders and organizations in the public, corporate, educational, and nonprofit sectors. Each year through its programs, the Center reaches more than twenty-seven thousand leaders and several thousand organizations worldwide. It also serves as a clearinghouse for ideas on leadership and creativity and regularly convenes conferences and colloquia by scholars and practitioners.

Funding primarily comes from tuition, sales of products and publications, royalties, and fees for service. The Center seeks grants and donations from corporations, foundations, and individuals in support of its educational mission.

For more information on the Center and its work, call Client Services at (336) 545-2810, send an e-mail to info@leaders.ccl.org, or visit the CCL World Wide Web home page at http://www.ccl.org.

CCL PRODUCTS, PROGRAMS AND PUBLICATIONS

The Center offers a variety of programs, products, and publications that help individuals, teams, and organizations learn about themselves.

Assessment Tools

Benchmarks® is a comprehensive 360-degree assessment tool that identifies strengths and development needs for middle to upper-middle managers and executives. Through the Benchmarks process, managers focus on skills, perspectives and values that research indicates they can learn and must learn to be effective as a leader. In addition, Benchmarks assesses potential derailment factors that can stall an otherwise promising career. In addition, the Benchmarks development process provides the opportunity to design a plan that links their development needs to specific experiences.

Skillscope® is a straightforward, effective, 360-degree feedback tool that assesses managerial strengths and development needs. It creates a channel through which managers and supervisors can get feedback from peers, direct reports, superiors, and bosses.

Prospector™ is designed to measure an individual's ability to learn and take advantage of growth experiences that will facilitate his or her development as a leader.

Keys® is a valid and reliable research-based tool that assesses the climate for creativity in a work group, division or organization. It measures both stimulants and barriers to creativity, as well as perceived productivity and creativity.

Programs

Leadership Development Program (LDP)® helps middle-level to upper-level managers and executives enhance their leadership skills in a variety of organizational settings, improve their ability to develop employees and promote excellence in all aspects of their lives.

Leadership Development for Human Resource Professionals helps participants become more effective and productive and, as leaders, assist others in achieving these goals.

Tools for Developing Successful Executives helps human resource executives, line managers, and career development professionals learn and apply some of CCL's best research-based, executive-development practices and tools.

Leading Creatively is designed to equip managers and executives with the creative competencies needed to make sense of, and deal more effectively with, the complexity and ambiguity of leadership in contemporary organizations.

The Women's Leadership Program helps women executives examine a wide range of issues affecting their roles and advancement in organizations, develop a deeper understanding of the forces that influence their lives and careers, and shape strategies for their development as individuals, professionals, and leaders.

Foundations of Leadership helps managers with 3 to 5 years experience whose roles increasingly include a leadership component requiring an ability to set and communicate a clear direction, motivate, provide coaching and feedback, and assist others in their organizations to succeed.

The African American Leadership Program provides mid- to senior-level African American managers with an open and candid environment in which to consider the forces influencing their professional performance and career advancement.

Leadership at the Peak gives top executives the opportunity, in a small but powerful group of peers, to evaluate themselves as leaders, gain new insights on topics that are important to them and their organizations, and focus on the challenges of leadership.

Publications

Readings in Innovation
Editors: Stanley S. Gryskiewicz and David A. Hills
This book provides a collection of articles to help today's managers understand and better utilize the innovation process.

International Success: Strategies for Selecting, Developing, and Supporting Expatriate Managers
Meena Wilson and Maxine A. Dalton
What is expatriate effectiveness and can the capabilities that contribute to it be developed? The authors address these questions and report the results of their research with 89 expatriates from the US, Europe, and the Middle East.

Ideas Into Action Guidebook Series
Series Editor: Russ Moxley
These guidebooks are designed to facilitate the practicing manager's ability to act. Each publication contains proven, practical actions for carrying out a specific developmental task or solving a specific leadership problem.

Stanley S. Gryskiewicz

Positive Turbulence

Developing Climates for
Creativity, Innovation, and Renewal

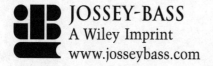

JOSSEY-BASS
A Wiley Imprint
www.josseybass.com

Center for
Creative Leadership

leadership. learning. life.

Published by Jossey-Bass
A Wiley Imprint
989 Market Street, San Francisco, CA 94103-1741   www.josseybass.com

Jossey-Bass books and products are available through most bookstores. To contact Jossey-Bass directly call our Customer Care Department within the U.S. at (800) 956-7739, outside the U.S. at (317) 572-3986 or fax (317) 572-4002.

Jossey-Bass also publishes its books in a variety of electronic formats. Some content that appears in print may not be available in electronic books.

Library of Congress Cataloging-in-Publication Data

Gryskiewicz, Stanley S.
Positive turbulence: developing climates for creativity, innovation, and renewal / by Stanley S. Gryskiewicz.–1st ed.
p. cm.
"A joint publication by the Jossey-Bass business & management series and the Center for Creative Leadership."
ISBN 0-7879-1008-2 (acid-free paper)
1. Creative ability in business. 2. Creative thinking. 3. Organizational change. I. Center for Creative Leadership. II. Title.
HD53 .G79 1999
658.4'06–dc21   99-6075

Printed in the United States of America
FIRST EDITION
HB Printing   10 9 8 7 6 5 4 3

A joint publication of

the Jossey-Bass Business & Management Series

and the Center for Creative Leadership

Contents

To Nur, Danielle, Kent, and Jon:
My family, and my Positive Turbulence

Preface

When I was a youngster back in the 1950s, my family purchased its first television, a rather small black-and-white set that seems primitive now but was magical then. One evening I watched, mesmerized, a drama that I have never forgotten. The story was a simple one, but its profound message has stayed with me through the years. In one sense, it has become a metaphor for the concepts of creativity and innovation that have been the focus of my professional life.

In this story, a Japanese fishing village in the nineteenth century has just been devastated by a tsunami, a large tidal wave. It is not a new occurrence; as long as anyone can remember, tsunamis have appeared from the sea without warning, destroying much of the village and killing many of the inhabitants. The villagers know that more tsunamis will come, always without warning, and they believe they can do nothing to predict or prevent them. They have learned to accept the inevitable with resignation.

As the story unfolds, one curious fact becomes clear: after each devastating tidal wave, the survivors rebuild their homes in the same place, along the beach. Even more curious, all the doorways and windows of the new huts are designed to face inland, away from the killer sea. The villagers have an active wish not to know when the inevitable will happen again.

The conflict at the heart of this drama concerns a young fisherman who decides to go against tradition and rebuild his home facing the ocean. He wants to know when the tsunami will come again. The rest of the community sees this as an act of great foolishness. Who would want to see death approaching? But the young fisherman, representing the new generation, wants to use his knowledge of the sea to guide his actions and protect his family.

To develop coping strategies for responding, the fisherman spends days looking out across the sea, noting occurrences and changes, trying to anticipate when the next storm will come and what will be the speed of the storm wave, the volume of water, and the intensity of the wind. Will it be a seasonal storm or a dragon-breathing tsunami?

The image of the fisherman has returned to me again and again over the years. There is much to be learned from his tale: Don't turn your back from the periphery, but look to it for the information you need. Ignoring the inevitability of change can be fatal. Learn from real-world events and adapt new strategies. Become a knight, not a pawn. Question the status quo.

Over the years I found myself applying many of those lessons to my own life and to companies with which I worked through the Center for Creative Leadership. The more useful those lessons came to be in my work, the more I found myself organizing them into a process that I eventually came to call Positive Turbulence— information critical for the long-term benefit of the organization and distinct from random and spurious turbulence, which is of no use and may even be detrimental.

The ideas for this process came from two major areas: research that I have done during and since graduate school, and experiences I have had these past thirty years working with a broad range of global companies that have experimented with and successfully implemented innovation and renewal.

In the mid-1970s when I did my graduate work at the University of London, I came across the writing of Michael Kirton. I was particularly struck by his approach to conceptualizing problem definition and creativity in terms of style, rather than measuring it quantitatively in terms of output or quantity alone (Kirton, 1976). In my thesis on group creative problem-solving techniques, I incorporated this idea to demonstrate that all of us are creative; we just differ in our personal style of creativity.

Around the same time, I was also influenced by the writings of Alex Osborn, one of the founders of the early advertising agency Batten, Barton, Durstine & Osborn (BBDO). He coined the term *brainstorming* and suggested that groups using his technique produced 44 percent more ideas than the same number of individuals working alone (Osborn, 1979). Subsequent findings by researchers, moreover, demonstrated that four or five people working alone but using brainstorming's deferred judgment principle produced more ideas than four or five people working on a team. When I applied Kirton's ideas about creativity style to team idea generation activities, I found that teams could be guided to find the most appropriate solution to a problem if they used the appropriate creativity style, which could be influenced by the group problem-solving activity they used. In the 1980s that concept was extended to the organizational level. Companies sought to include and manage the different styles of creativity in what can be described as bilateral organizations, which seek to manage well both radical and incremental innovations.

At the same time that I was keeping up with studies on creativity, I was also following the literature on applied psychology, more specifically, assessment for personal development. This literature encompassed the influence of the 1960s' human potential movement and its focus on self-awareness as being the starting place for human development and personal change.

By the early 1980s, I saw how personnel departments were incorporating the principles of that movement into their guidance of their organizations. If individual members can develop and change once they become aware of the impact their behavior has on others, they reasoned, then that knowledge can be used to improve the overall organization.

Around the same time, teams were becoming ubiquitous in corporations—cross-functional, self-managing, product development, project management, quality improvement, manufacturing, and even executive teams. Systems thinking, another paradigm of note, then shifted to looking at the idea that individuals and teams could be only as successful as the organization's culture allowed. Assessment for development now included assessing the organization's culture and climate.

The next decade brought chaos theory—searching for order in disorder, predictability in the seemingly unpredictable. Now companies looked at information or influences not just inside but also outside the organization.

As you will see as you read further, all of these ideas and theories helped me shape the concepts for Positive Turbulence. By looking at chaos theory, in particular, I saw the need to focus on the periphery of the organization to bring in the turbulence necessary for change. In teams I saw an intact unit for practicing Positive Turbulence and saw how a number of team practices could also be applied to the organization as a whole. In considering different styles of creativity, I saw the need not just to use those different styles but also to invite multiple perspectives into organizations and to embrace change. From the systems thinking studies into culture and climate, I saw how essential it was to establish the appropriate climate if receptivity to Positive Turbulence were to be achieved.

Simultaneous with this research were the real-world experiences I have had working with a whole range of international corporations, from those in the service industry, such as the Scandinavian Airlines System, to those in sales and manufacturing, such as the Goodyear Tire & Rubber Co., Milliken & Company, and the Mead Corporation. A substantial portion of my experience comes from the consumer products, transportation, and pharmaceutical industries, working with Unilever, S. C. Johnson & Son, Norfolk Southern Corporation, Pfizer, Nortel Networks, and Hallmark Cards.

Through my work with these organizations I saw that when companies desire to maintain industry leadership, they are fully committed to seeking a constant flow of creative ideas and new products and processes. In all of these cases I saw that many of the theories I had been exploring were being put into practice, so I was able to evaluate them to see how effective they were. Those practices that worked, I sought to have implemented in appropriate

ways in other organizations. At each stage, I refined my thinking
and methods, until I evolved the ideas and mechanisms for Positive Turbulence that I explain in this book.

I wrote this book precisely because the information I present in
it had not been gathered together and codified, and there was a need
for this to be done. When I introduced the concepts of Positive Turbulence to different companies they were so favorably received and
applied that I knew they could be of value to thousands of other
organizations looking to maintain a competitive edge.

As for the fisherman in the story, he survived a number of
tsunamis, whereas many of his fellow villagers did not. By scanning
the far edges of the unpredictable sea, he learned to read the signs
indicating an impending tsunami. By embracing change and going
against the status quo, he was able to find a coping strategy that
enabled him to survive longer than he might otherwise. He could
not take control of the turbulent sea—that was impossible—but he
managed his responses to it in the most effective ways, using the
new information he was continually absorbing to guide his responses.
That is what Positive Turbulence is all about.

Whether you lead or are a manager in a very large, multibillion-
dollar international sales and manufacturing corporation, a mid-
sized regional service company, or a national firm dealing with
intellectual property, many of the ideas discussed in this book will
be applicable to your organization. I hope that in reading it you will
learn to translate the mechanisms of Positive Turbulence for use
in your own organization so that it can experience continuous
renewal and success.

Acknowledgments

It is time to acknowledge the people, the institutions, and the experiences that have contributed to the ideas contained in this book. I have stood on the shoulders of giants, I have bounced ideas off colleagues, and I have learned from my experiences with clients. The experiences I have had are more numerous than those captured between the covers of this book.

David Hills, my graduate school professor, has continued to support and tutor me during my professional years and helped formulate the ideas around Positive Turbulence. Both David and Martin Wilcox, the director of publications at CCL, are supportive colleagues who get as excited as I do about the ideas contained inside *Positive Turbulence*.

Maggie Stuckey provided the initial conception of the organization of the manuscript. She gave invaluable help in highlighting major themes.

Karen Sharpe played a pivotal role in making this an effective manuscript. She refined the structure and edited and sculpted my less sharply focused outpourings. Her work was invaluable, too.

These four helped with the structure of the book and the written expression of the ideas. Editors are talented people who are not often recognized for their contributions. Only writers who have made themselves vulnerable to the editing process understand the valued role of the editor—the sensitive editor. I want to acknowledge these four sensitive idea communicators.

My clients who also became friends should be acknowledged:

Joe Gelmini	David Welty	Bob Rosenfeld
Dale Shackle	Dick Wright	Bruce Wright
John Rampey	Mike Malone	Ingar Skaug

Their experiences, which they shared with me, helped provide the glue of the real world.

Thanks to David Campbell, Kenneth Clark, Walter Ulmer, and John Red, I was able to be a part of a Positive Turbulence–driven group within the Center for Creative Leadership, entitled Innovation and Creativity Applications and Research (ICAR). I would like to acknowledge the contributions the following professionals have made to this work:

Donald MacKinnon	Teresa Amabile	George Davies
Luke Novelli	Robert Burnside	Jim Shields
Sylvester Taylor	Anne Faber	Michael Kirton
Richard Hackman	Bob Bacon	Bob Dorn
Roald Nomme	Jim Bruce	David Horth
Elizabeth Holmes	Per Groholt	Karen Boylston
Harlan Cleveland	Ben Gantz	Sid Parnes

None of this work would have happened if the Center for Creative Leadership had not been supported by the Richardson family: H. Smith Richardson Jr. and Peter Richardson. Thank you for tolerating the fuzzy front end of our creative thinking.

The following people suggested that my experiences should be captured in book form as a means to reach a wider audience:

Bob Lee	John Alexander	David DeVries
Larry Alexander	Byron Schneider	

I must acknowledge Lu Noe, who helped keep the Word documents straight and me sane.

I acknowledge all those Generation Xers who keep me up and running.

I acknowledge all those who made contributions to the content of this book along the way: Peggy Cartner, David Kennard,

Betty Zimmerman, John Old, Al Vergona, Caroline Paoletti, Sandra Dudley, Bobby Bradford, Nur Dokur Gryskiewicz, Bill Shea, John McKeithan, Susan Rice, Carol Andresen, Walter Griggs, Jim Channon, John Cimino and my friends at Associated Solo Artists, Marita Wesely-Clough, Fred Trussell, Morgan McCall, Michael Lombardo, Bill Drath, K. Larry Hastie, David Tanner, Mary Wallgren, Elizabeth "Libby" Larsen, Fred Reichley, Danielle Gryskiewicz, Chapin Kaynor, Noriaki Kadota, Bob Nalewajek, Julian Mount, and Joanne Ferguson.

I acknowledge those who provided cultural insights and translations of the concept "manage change before change manages you": Fisan Bankale, Sevim Yalciner, Nelia Garcia-Yurcisin, Beth Gegner, Meena Surie Wilson, Ece Kutay, Adel Safty, Zehra and Yalcin Suer, Patrick Colemont, Pedro Tavares, Michael Makale, Inna Il'yasova Tuttle, Bakh Malak, and Zack Williams.

Thank you, each of you, for the Positive Turbulence you have provided me.

The Author

Stanley S. Gryskiewicz, a vice president of global initiatives and senior fellow in creativity and innovation at the Center for Creative Leadership, Greensboro, North Carolina, is an international authority in innovation with thirty years of experience. He has investigated—through both research and application—innovation in new product development, team creativity, and service delivery in the United States, Canada, South America, Europe, Egypt, Australia, New Zealand, Japan, and Korea. Gryskiewicz, whose Ph.D. is in organizational psychology from the University of London, has been at the Center for Creative Leadership since its inception in 1970. Prior to being named senior fellow in creativity and innovation in 1991, he helped develop the Center's Leadership Development Program and led in the formation of the innovation and creativity applications and research area. He has worked with the Japan Management Association in Japan, the World Bank in the United States, the United Nations University/International Leadership Academy in Jordan, the Moscow G. V. Plekhanov Institute of National Economy in Russia, and Sundridge Park in the United Kingdom and with companies such as Pfizer International, Hewlett-Packard, Bank of Montreal, Nortel Networks, the *New York Times,* Norfolk Southern Corporation, S. C. Johnson, Novartis, Merck, Lucent, Glaxo Research Institute, Unilever, Marithe & François Girbaud, Goodyear International, Willis Corroon Group, Scandinavian Airlines Systems, and Champion International—in addition to numerous trade associations and academic institutions.

Introduction

Browse through the business section of almost any bookstore, and you are bound to find dozens of books on creativity and its offspring, innovation. Read any business journal or news magazine, and you are likely to find articles on these subjects appearing with a predictable regularity. The reason is that creativity and innovation have been found to be the cornerstones of healthy organizations that are ready for reinventing themselves. Organizations do this by being relevant to changing markets and making use of new technology. I call this process renewal.

When employees are enveloped by a creative environment, they are free to puzzle over new information and creative ideas and implement successful and innovative solutions, plans, and projects. Given the fast-changing world we live in today, companies need precisely this kind of process and supportive climate to adapt and thrive in the long term.

As I have observed and worked with organizations over the past thirty years, it has become increasingly apparent to me that the most effective groups were the ones in which creativity flourished. In some of these places, the environment that caused that to happen was unplanned; in others it had been brilliantly implanted into the organization's fiber.

In such places I might find small teams tossing around crazy ideas for an upcoming project. Or I might see people of all different ages and levels and backgrounds somewhat rowdily generating ideas in a common work area. Or I might find individuals still in their offices at well past midnight poring through seemingly unrelated books, Web sites, and periodicals struggling in the quest for the new.

Creativity does not have to be random. Organizational structures can, in fact, be put in place that provide for a more predictable, ongoing occurrence of innovation and renewal. This book is about setting up those structures through a process that begins with the recognition that change is inevitable, and then uses change, in manageable amounts, to the organization's strategic advantage. I call this process Positive Turbulence.

Turbulence is energetic, forceful, catalytic, unpredictable. It can be unsettling. Spreadsheets showing a devastating fourth quarter, reports of a competitor's secret new product, layoffs, and the merging of two divisions can cause unhinging in a company.

Yet often that can be a good thing. The dreadful fourth quarter could cause the company to take measures it would never have considered before that might ultimately lead it in a new and profitable direction. The competitor's new project might suggest that it is time for a shift in focus at the company, and this could result in rewarding new endeavors. The merger of two divisions, with the potential for a cross-fertilization of ideas, could very well result in totally unforeseen initiatives.

What is needed to turn the turbulence into a positive force is knowledge management. This means putting structures in place for bringing in new information, making sense of it, and turning it into novel ideas that are useful and eventually can be implemented. "Residing out on the periphery of the organization today are the ideas which will revolutionize the organization tomorrow," said Dee Hock (1998), founder and CEO emeritus of Visa International, in a speech before Vice President Al Gore's Reinventing the Government Task Force's Reinvention Revolution Conference.

This process takes advantage of the ubiquitous turbulence found on an organization's periphery and brings some of it to center stage to be examined and used in a structured way. The external turbulence is then filtered, evaluated, and finally internalized, creating a controlled state of Positive Turbulence. The result is a resonance within the organization that stimulates innovation and renewal in a way that the process from information to creative idea to innovation and renewal repeats itself.

"The most creative thing occurs at the meeting places of disciplines," said Mary Catherine Bateson in *Composing a Life* (1990). "At the center of any tradition, it is easy to become blind to alternatives. At the edges, where lines are blurred, it is easier to imagine that the world might be different. Vision and new direction sometimes arise from confusion."

Chapter One explains why Positive Turbulence is necessary in companies, beginning with an examination of the fast-changing workplace that businesses face, and then seeing how turbulence, skillfully ushered into an organization, can be turned into a positive force for continuous renewal.

The four key elements that drive Positive Turbulence are explored in Chapter Two: difference (breaking out of the status quo), multiple perspectives (inviting divergent viewpoints and nontraditional interpretations), intensity (keeping the speed, volume, and force of the turbulence at an optimal level for change), and receptivity (providing mechanisms for individuals to be able to thrive in an environment driven by Positive Turbulence).

Chapter Three looks specifically at strategies that companies can implement for increasing receptivity to Positive Turbulence— ways that employees can broaden their knowledge and experiences, what they can do to reinvigorate their thinking, and how companies can mitigate some of the barriers to and undesired consequences of Positive Turbulence.

Teams are suitable units for developing Positive Turbulence because they are breeding grounds for creativity. We look in Chapter Four at what constitutes a team, discuss strategies that teams can adopt for developing Positive Turbulence, and consider the role of a turbulence-driven team in a turbulence-averse company.

The strategies that companies can undertake to manage Positive Turbulence, from using the periphery most propitiously to developing the appropriate corporate culture to ensuring that the turbulence remains positive, are covered in Chapter Five.

Finally, Chapter Six gives a sense of the whole picture with real-world examples of Positive Turbulence in action. We look at three very different companies—Norfolk Southern, Hallmark, and 3M (Minnesota Mining and Manufacturing)—that all follow the practices of Positive Turbulence. Although these companies go about it in very different ways, they share a common outcome of continuous renewal.

Positive Turbulence is a marvelous process that breaks through the walls reinforcing the status quo and rushes in with new information and novel ideas to reinvigorate companies on a sustainable basis.

Chapter One

The Case for Positive Turbulence

In the 1950s the typical business organization was a monolith that valued nothing so much as predictability and repeatability. In the name of efficiency, companies were system-designed to maintain order and reduce variability. In the environment of the time, this "keep it the same and everyone will be happy" approach made a certain kind of sense. Competition was nonexistent, and customers were content to receive whatever the companies supplied. Employees, happy to have a steady job and a regular paycheck, made few demands on employers.

Today's business climate is entirely different. Social change, foreign competition, deregulation, environmental issues, global economic forces, and mind-boggling technology have turned the stability of forty years ago on its head, leaving a new world that is unpredictable, and sometimes terrifyingly so. Many business leaders try to cope by seeking to impose order, organization, and focus, but at a high price: a lack of innovation. And with strictures and narrow thinking comes a loss of creativity. This is not the way to adapt to the changes taking place today. What is needed instead is to see in new ways, come up with new approaches, and veer off into different directions. And this can be done only in an organization that values variance and change and knows how to use them to its strategic advantage.

This is where Positive Turbulence comes in. Based on a counterintuitive notion—using turbulence to organize the chaos out on the edges of the organization—it offers a process for turning change into a productive force that, properly managed, can lead to innovation and ongoing renewal. It recognizes that variances can be the building blocks for the future, it sees that information and ideas from the periphery of the organization are the source for creativity and innovation, it embraces change as the ideal way to meet the challenges of a complex world, and it points the direction and sets the pace for ongoing renewal.

Looking at Today's Fast-Changing Workplace

Today's workplace is in such a state of flux that even those who never experienced the placidity of the 1950s find it hard to keep up. Competition has become fierce with the constant introduction of lower-cost labor and goods. Social changes have presented businesses with splintered markets that reflect a complex new generation of global consumers. If they have any hope of keeping up, organizations must be capable of changing direction quickly and appropriately to meet the demands of an increasingly fickle marketplace.

On top of that, the pace of change is accelerating rapidly. Manufacturers of information products now have to assume that their devices, programs, or processes have a shelf half-life of about three months. Upgrade twice a year or fall behind. Ship an entirely new product line every eighteen months or die. Manufacturers of traditional consumer products are discovering that the familiar ten-year lag from basic research to product development to organizational implementation seems an anachronistic luxury.

To make matters worse, companies cannot wait for consumers to tell them what they want; sometimes consumers themselves do not know. As a further complication, business organizations cannot even take their workforce for granted. Today's employees are demanding more than pay and benefits; they want to be listened to, and they want to participate in the decisions that affect them directly. They want work to be a fulfilling part of their lives, and they do not hesitate to change jobs to find that fulfillment.

Some organizations find that this new environment is too frenetic, too unfamiliar, too complex, too hard to get a grip on. Faced with paralyzing uncertainty, their first instinct is to try to restore some sense of control. So they turn inward and look for mechanisms that provide order, organization, and focus. The problem is that these mechanisms often put a damper on creativity.

Traditional business organizations have long been managed in a manner that reduces variance. Even recent management trends such as total quality initiatives and reengineering and redesign are, at their core, attempts to reduce uncertainty. Following the thinking that any variance represents inefficiency and thus a cost to be dealt with, these traditional companies have as their underlying goal the elimination of variances and maintenance of control. Their year plans often conclude with the following statement: "There will be no surprises."

Unfortunately, when organizations eliminate the source of variances, they also eliminate the source of innovation. Trying to "keep everything the same," they unwittingly keep out the fresh ideas on which their future depends. Remember what happened to International Business Machines (IBM). Its attachment to the mainframe computer and emphasis on sales and finance rather than on the leading-edge technology in its own laboratories led to its loss of market share. The insulated top management at General Motors Corporation (GM) did not understand the significance and potential impact of Japanese competition and customers' demands for quality, safety, and economy; it had not had to. It too lost market share—in this case, to Honda, Toyota, and Volvo, companies that experimented with new manufacturing concepts and looked at fresh market information from a variety of sources.

Intel Corporation is a company that knows the value of variance. In 1985, amid increasing competition from Japanese memory chip makers, it decided to change its strategic direction significantly and focus on the microprocessor business. In pondering this huge decision, Andrew Grove, Intel's president and chief operating officer, posed a hypothetical question to Gordon Moore, the company's chair and chief executive officer: "If we got kicked out and the board brought in a new CEO, what do you think he would do?" Moore responded by saying "he would get us out of memories." Grove shot back, "Why shouldn't you and I walk out the door, come back, and do it ourselves?" They did. Grove and Moore instituted drastic corporate transformations, closing eight Intel memory chip plants, cutting the workforce by 30 percent, and reducing salaries (Bradenberger and Nalebuff, 1996). Having refashioned its corporate strategy around the microprocessor, by the 1990s it was leading the microprocessor industry in new directions (Young, 1996). What made these radical moves possible was that Intel, unlike GM or IBM, had certain structures and policies in place for working with change. Constructive confrontation, whereby Intel employees were encouraged to challenge any other employee regardless of managerial rank, was one. Fast and open communication among and between employees at all levels was another (Hof, 1995).

What Intel, Honda, and the Gap, which outmaneuvered the staid Sears, Roebuck and Co., had in common is that they took the turbulence that was on the edge or already a part of their organizations and transformed it into a positive force.

Turning Turbulence into a Positive Force

Eric Trist (Emery and Trist, 1965), an English psychologist, first used the term *turbulence* to describe the constantly changing environment in which modern organizations must operate. The term usually has a negative connotation; in the course of human affairs, as in the natural world, turbulence is generally associated with some kind of trouble—at best an annoyance, at worst a tragic disaster.

Yet that chaotic, swirling, frenetic environment that threatens to drown us all is also where new trends are incubated. Out of the disruption, change, and chaos brought about by turbulence always comes useful information. The problem is how to sort through and capture it without swamping the boat. Out of the upheaval caused by the disbanding of a marketing department, its members disbursed to other areas of the company, will come the new perspectives and fresh ideas that those former marketeers bring to their new departments. But if these individuals are left unguided, their efforts disregarded or even dismissed, the company loses out on the valuable information and ideas they have to offer.

Here is the good news: by deliberately bringing in turbulence, organizations are actually creating stability. When management sees new trends early and brings them inside and works with them, they are guarding against being blindsided. Because they know ahead of time what is going to be important, there are fewer crises and no surprises. The sharp spikes of radical change are eliminated, and the organization achieves balance.

Just as turbulence exists and will continue to exist on the high seas and in air currents above land, it exists and will continue to exist in companies and organizations, large and small. Companies that view a turbulent environment as an ominous whirlpool must learn to see it as a reservoir teeming with new ideas. The challenge is to sort through and channel the turbulence and turn it into a positive force for renewal. That process is set in motion by welcoming variances, expanding the field of vision, and embracing change.

Seeing Variances as Building Blocks for the Future

Most organizations strive for consistency and agreement. They feel that by conducting their business and running their organization with no allowances for divergence, they can help ensure ongoing success. We have all known managers and executives who seem to have a narcissistic need to have everyone tell them they are doing a great job, doing everything just right. We have known others who feel they need to run a tight ship, with everyone in accord and no challenges to their authority. Those who disagree with them too often usually find dismissal letters in their mailboxes. What occurs when that person with whom everyone must agree happens to be wrong is analogous to what happens when the goose leading the flock in V-formation hits a bad air current or low-flying aircraft: all the other geese follow along, and they all go down together.

Diversity, varied viewpoints, different styles, dissenting opinions: all of these variances are necessary if a company is to renew itself and move ahead. The survival of a company does not depend so much on the degree to which the employees see eye-to-eye with their managers, except, of course, with regard to some core values like honesty and fairness and agreement as to what their strategic goals are. But it does often depend on the degree to which people disagree with one another, or even seek contradictory data, for out of respectful dissension come the creative ideas that form the basis for company growth.

Think back to when you or someone else came up with a new plan or program or project, and coworkers argued its merits. Undoubtedly everyone found the discussion useful in helping to clarify thinking, revise the plan, come up with an alternative solution, or confirm the direction proposed. You may have felt good about the comments that praised the project, but you probably learned much more from those who challenged and questioned it. It is these challenges that can help strengthen a plan by giving it a much more solid foundation. Organizations that consider variances as costs that need to be controlled must begin to think of them instead as building blocks of the future.

The role of variances in a turbulence-driven organization is to generate turbulence. The different ways of doing and thinking and seeing contribute to the energetic, vibrant, dynamic atmosphere in which creativity can thrive. To bring variances consciously into an organization often requires looking beyond the organization by scanning the periphery for new ideas.

Focusing on the Periphery as the Source for Innovation and Renewal

Think of the periphery as an amorphous place beyond the confines of the organization from whence comes new information as low-frequency signals. These signals, which may be signs of new trends (in the marketplace, for example) or winds of change (such as technology shifts), then come into the organization, stirring things up, creating turbulence, engendering innovation, and leading to renewal.

Hartness International, a manufacturer of case-packing machines, had heard of videoconferencing capabilities that a company called PictureTel had developed (Salter, 1998). Looking for a way that it could service its customers' malfunctioning machines without actually having to travel to the customer's site, Hartness thought that perhaps PictureTel could help. Together the two companies developed the Video Response System, which allows Hartness engineers, sitting in their home office, to actually "see" the malfunctioning machines via videoconference and handle the majority of its customer service calls within minutes rather than days. By paying attention to new information sitting out on the periphery of technology, Hartness devised an innovative and highly effective solution.

Every big trend starts as a small, one-of-a-kind blip on the screen, easy to overlook and easy to dismiss. Only those paying close attention to the turbulent periphery will see it, and only those predisposed to thinking that turbulence can be positive will see its strategic potential. The task for visionary leaders is to create an environment where new information is embraced, not feared. On a tactical level, this means establishing mechanisms for finding new information and ushering it into the organization (we examine more closely how to do this in Chapter Three), and then putting that new information into the hands of people who can best make sense of it. This is all key to the process of Positive Turbulence.

A few years ago I witnessed a powerful demonstration of the importance of periphery during a Creativity Week hosted by the Center for Creative Leadership. For this event, we invited cutting-edge thinkers and artists to test before an audience of creativity practitioners their current thinking, along with an experiential exercise designed to drive home the theory. At this particular presentation, Thomas Sayre, a sculptor, gave a group of managers a new way to think about organizational change.

First he dimmed the lights in the auditorium to about the level of nightfall, and asked the audience to continue looking straight ahead as if he were still addressing them from the podium. Then he quietly walked halfway down the side aisle and lit a match.

"Did you see that?" he asked.

Since the match was in the peripheral vision of almost all those in the audience, they answered, "Of course."

"Then use it. That's your periphery, and at the moment it's the only source of light." He went on to explain, with the passion of an artist, his view that information found on the periphery is the key to new ideas. It is folly to ignore the periphery and pay attention only to the mainstream; after all, everything that is now a current issue or new product was once on the periphery.

Out on the edge, this side of chaos, lie the early warning signs that are already present, signs of potential dangers, such as the Y2K problem, proposed new tax legislation, new market opportunities, developing trends. But the signs are weak, and only those who are paying attention can see and understand them. Learning to detect weak signals in the distance helps the astute organization to recognize the once unrecognizable. Learning to do so ahead of the competition provides the strategic advantage that can ensure survival.

What becomes immediately clear is that organizations that consciously decide to tune in to these far-off, fuzzy, intermittent signals get critical information faster than those who wait for it to arrive in a neat, orderly bandwidth. By the time the trends are obvious, the competition has noticed and has already begun retooling.

Consider what happened to the large integrated steel companies in this country—Bethlehem Steel Corporation and U.S. Steel, for example. They failed to pay attention to a number of events that were happening on the periphery. They did not see, or they ignored, the challenge posed by mini-mills, such as Nucor Corporation, that were able to provide product at lower cost partly due to more advanced technological techniques (Preston, 1991). They did not see, or they disregarded, management trends, such as flattened organizations with incentive systems, that also helped their competition surge ahead, to the degree that Nucor is today the number three steel producer in the United States. To avoid such blindsiding, companies need to expand their vision, taking in as much of the periphery as they can.

Siemens AG is a company that does just that. It pays careful attention to "the main competitive challenges [coming] from companies alien to established industries," according to Claus Weyrich (Teresko, 1997), senior vice president for corporate technology. Such attention to the periphery, along with other strategies related to the practice of Positive Turbulence, have enabled Siemens to survive for a century and a half and be an industry leader. A banner celebrating the company's birthday said, "150 years of growth through innovation."

Consciously and purposely opening up the organization's boundaries to allow new information in is a basic tenet of Positive Turbulence because Positive Turbulence is all about a shift in organizational mind-set, away from focusing solely on what is inside the organization today. It is no longer enough to concentrate on making the current product better or cheaper or faster or shinier; leaders need to open up their thinking in all ways, even if some of what comes in seems strange or murky as to what to do with it.

My former graduate school psychology professor, David Hills, an intellectual free spirit with a one-of-a-kind mind, has often contributed sketches and cartoons for activities at the Center for Creative Leadership and finds just the right way of visually conveying abstract or complex ideas. I have been lecturing about Positive Turbulence for some time, and I know that it can seem abstract. Dave Hills came to the rescue with two illustrations, one showing a traditional organization (Figure 1.1), the other showing an organization in which Positive Turbulence operates (Figure 1.2).

Looking at the Traditional Organization. The big rectangle in Figure 1.1 represents the organization and the small circles within it the people. The people are grouped into rigid teams of various sizes (the larger circles). Most of the teams have a person who functions as leader—either a designated leader (small square) or an informal leader (star).

Figure 1.1. Traditional Organization

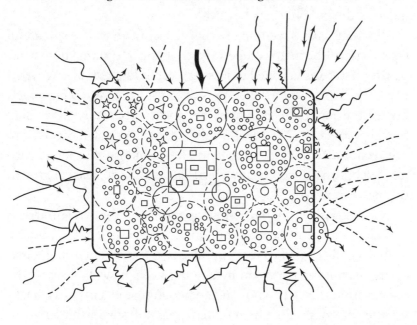

In an actual company the large circles would be the different departments where all members keep to their tasks, focusing on the job at hand. The departments have little interaction with one another, and there is negligible sharing of information. These larger circles might also represent work groups within a department and function in the same insular, myopic way as the department.

The arrows are the bits and pieces of new information in the external environment; some is obvious (solid lines), some subtle (dotted lines). But the organization is very tight, very structured, and there is no room for flexibility or change. The walls, which are solid, suggest the company culture that mandates sticking to the tried-and-true, avoiding anything from outside the mainstream, resisting anything different.

Except for one place designated for access, the port at the very top, all the arrows are being repelled by the solid barrier—the company's rigidity of thinking that prevents new ideas from being considered. Even the port is guarded by a large group that acts as the

Figure 1.2. Turbulence-Driven Organization

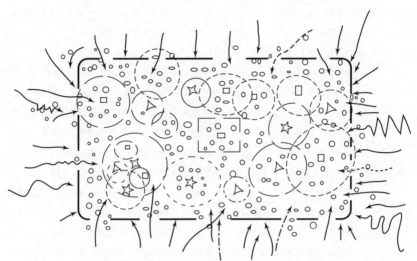

gatekeeper for information; its job is to buffer new information from senior management. The limitations of their thinking and perceiving guide the organization.

Looking at a Turbulence-Driven Organization. Figure 1.2 reveals a very different situation: an organization where Positive Turbulence thrives. As you can see, there is more space, more flexibility. Teams are loosely configured, some overlapping with others, and people freely move in and out of them. The senior management group is not boxed in; these managers interact with others at all different levels of the company. And most important of all, the boundaries of the organization are open; information flows in at many points and is captured by many different people, who take it in many directions. Some of the organization's members even move outside the border to the broader environment, searching for even better ideas.

Information coming in from the periphery, the near side of chaos, may well be experienced as chaotic. Charles II of England certainly discovered that to be the case after he granted the Royal Society, the world's first professional association of scientists, its first charter in 1662, and all he saw this august group doing was meeting and debating—"debating nothing," he claimed. As it happened, they were discussing the concept of vacuum, a perplexing idea that came from outside the society and provoked much discussion within it (Polanyi, 1994).

The early thinking of that group is today known as vacuum science, and it provided the understanding for the development of barometers, pumps, hot-air balloons, steam engines, light bulbs, vacuum tubes, dried foods, and much more. If King Charles had forbidden such thinking and such drawing from the periphery, think of the developments that might never have come about.

Often, as this story shows, the usefulness of early thinking can be assessed only after a related discovery has been made. That is because to many in the organization, the outside information may seem bizarre, outrageous, weird; in their discomfiture, they may discount it as being of no practical value. In some cases, this is nothing more psychologically complex than fear of change. But squashing new ideas because they seem strange, or setting up barriers to protect against the "disruption" of outside forces, puts the organization at immediate risk of becoming outdated and left behind in the marketplace.

By broadening the field of vision to take in the valuable lessons and messages and information that reside outside the organization, or that lie buried in recesses within the organization, companies pave the way for coming up with innovative new approaches, for going off into a different direction, for branching out. To do that, they need to welcome change.

Embracing Change

Change happens in a series of irregular waves, some more disruptive than others. In my view, it makes more sense for organizations to face change in a structured, planned manner than to be continuously cobbling together one-of-a-kind responses to each wave. The concept of Positive Turbulence provides such a structure.

Positive Turbulence thrives as an energizing climate, one that upsets the status quo and impels people toward change. It is a culture purposefully engineered by leaders who recognize the need to create an environment compatible with change and peopled by organizational members who can adapt to the change opportunity. It provides stimuli to motivated, intelligent people who are looking for ways to make a contribution. We can think of it as a culture of improvisation, gleefully inviting in the unexpected.

Oddly enough, organizations that have been very successful in their fields often find it most difficult to change. Even though their historic success may have been built on a highly innovative idea, there is a common tendency to calcification: "We've been doing just fine with what we have; let's not mess with it." Any business leader tempted to follow that kind of thinking is cautioned to remember what happened to the railroads.

In 1960, in a groundbreaking *Harvard Business Review* article that quickly became a classic and was republished fifteen years later (Levitt, 1975), Theodore Levitt used the American railroad industry to describe a particularly destructive kind of organizational myopia. The railroads, he wrote, saw themselves as being in the railroad business rather than the transportation business. That kind of limited perspective was reinforced with several self-deceiving beliefs: that an expanding population ensures growth; that there is no competitive substitute for a major product; that the corporation should focus on making that one product better. By seeing itself solely in the railroad business, it kept its eyes narrowly focused on the tracks, and so it did not consider using trucks instead of boxcars or transporting information rather than coal.

The railroads had forcefully demolished their original competition—the horse and buggy—and were so certain of continued success that railroad owners were totally blind to the ramifications of the advent of automobiles, trucks, and airplanes. Not until their customers had enthusiastically embraced them did the railroads see them as legitimate alternative modes of transportation. By then it was too late.

Coca Cola, a successful multinational company and an American icon, is at the other extreme. Facing competition from not just Pepsi but mineral waters and juices, it needed to make a significant change. And so, as Ram Charan and Noel Tichy point out in their book *Every Business Is a Growth Business* (1998), the company broadened its view of the competition to include not only soft drinks but fluids in general—"winning a larger share of a huge opportunity." Its sales soared.

It is important to keep in mind that embracing change requires careful attention. Reliability, efficiency, recovery of development costs, and the generation of profits must be considered. Once any innovation is in place, a company does want to automate, optimize, regiment, and reduce variation and unplanned deviations. While railroads were efficient at standardizing and rigidly following optimal routines to achieve the essential goal, they did not set aside resources to go to the periphery and search for renewal options.

Avoiding the Trap of Success.   Whenever a company is stuck in "success" mode—that is, everyone thinks things are going great—that is the time of most danger. The very skills and behaviors that lead to success can become a trap. Those behaviors become so ingrained that the company can no longer see when it is time to rethink, to look for new approaches. What its leaders must do at that point is create a sense of restlessness, of urgently looking ahead for symptoms of marketplace change. (In Chapter Three we look at some of the ways to do that.)

You might think that airlines, also being in the transportation industry, would not make the same mistake as the railroads did. Yet what we are talking about here is being able to see through the clouds and understand what is there. Just a few years ago, did the strategic planners at commercial airlines imagine they would be competing for the business-travel dollar with an upstart copy center franchise? Of course not; they would not think to look in that direction.

Yet today people can drive to their local Kinko's Copy Center, with its videoconferencing capability, and conduct face-to-face meetings with customers in other cities who have access to similar technology. It is no longer necessary to fly to the customer's site, and airlines are feeling the pinch. A recent survey of 450 Fortune 1000 companies conducted by the National Business Travel Association (McDowell, 1998) indicated that 56 percent of the companies sampled have cut back the number of employees who travel, and 53 percent are using videoconferencing and teleconferencing to replace some of the travel. Airlines are scrambling to keep business travelers by upgrading business-class services and making phoning, faxing, and e-mailing onboard much easier.

The airlines are reacting to technological developments that affect their industry; instead they should have been anticipating and acting accordingly. That is what Virgin Atlantic Airlines did. "We didn't want to get in the transportation industry; we're still in the entertainment industry—at 25,000 feet," said Richard Branson (Peters, 1997), chair of the Virgin Group of Companies. Virgin has magicians and masseuses and videos at each seat on many of its flights, and Range Rover limousine service at Heathrow Airport provides an extension of service beyond the airport. Branson anticipates what the customer wants and provides it, keeping the competition off balance. He translates what he sees his customers wanting while on the ground to offerings he makes available in the air.

When a company avoids the trap of success and continuously searches for new ideas and new information, it is constantly renewing itself in accordance with the future world in which it must successfully operate.

Seeking Continuous Renewal. What we have come to call continuous renewal depends in large measure on an environment of Positive Turbulence. Without new information, there is no source for new ideas; without new ideas, organizations have no basis for taking action toward innovation; without innovation, future market share is lost, and companies die a slow and painful death. It is not an exaggeration to say that in many industries, renewal equals survival. Any organization that intends to compete in the years ahead must embrace the turbulence within which blow the winds of renewal.

Renewal is an active and deliberate process. Leaders must realize that neither the organization's history nor its immediate legacy will guarantee long-term survival. Renewal is dependent on the leader courageously making choices based on the accuracy of the novel information being presented, selected, and used. Positive Turbulence offers a structured format for an ongoing organizational renewal process that cautiously gleans from the perceived chaos the important message that is sometimes hidden in the incoming data. When people have access to information, they can grasp new opportunities for renewal at even the most dispersed levels of the organization. Choice, not avoidance, is the only active decision making available to leaders to bring about renewal.

To paraphrase Harlan Cleveland (1997), a political scientist, public servant, and current president of the World Academy of Art and Science, accelerated change is the destiny of the leaders of the future. It will not be an easy role to fill. Finding their way through complexity and making decisions along the way will require access to information that comes through open channels of Positive Turbulence. The leader's function will be to make difficult yet correct choices. In any society or organization, "those who choose the most have the most reason to feel free," Cleveland has said. With the freedom and knowledge to choose new and changing pathways comes the possibility for sustainable renewal.

———

Positive Turbulence is quite a simple idea. It does not require a dramatic, earthshaking change—nothing nearly as severe as reengineering the organization. It does require that those assigned to think about the long-term viability of the organization have the resources needed to keep their eyes on its peripheral environment, keep an open mind, and embrace considered change.

One thing is certain: into the foreseeable future all business organizations will operate in an atmosphere of turbulence. This environmental turbulence is inevitable, and it will intensify. Organizations must learn to operate in a world beset with as-yet-unseen gathering storms. The best of them will, like the young Japanese fisherman, face the chaos head on, looking for early signs of change that they can shape to their advantage. Positive Turbulence offers them a means to do just that.

Chapter Two

The Dynamics of Positive Turbulence

Positive Turbulence is a paradoxical process: you invite an energizing, disparate, invigorating, unpredictable force into your organization so that you can use its chaotic energy and direct it toward continuous renewal. You create an environment that upsets the status quo and impels people toward change.

Four key elements are the motivating forces behind Positive Turbulence: difference, multiple perspectives, intensity, and receptivity. *Difference* relates to breaking out of the status quo by incorporating programs that do not resemble what has been done formerly, by bringing in information that is unexpected. *Multiple perspectives*—divergent viewpoints, nontraditional interpretations—are needed to get people seeing, thinking, and acting in new ways. Encouraging difference and inviting multiple perspectives create the greatest opportunities for an outbreak of novel ideas. *Intensity* is the speed, volume, and force of the turbulence. The organization's ability to manage the intensity appropriately makes the difference between turbulence that is positive and turbulence that is negative. *Receptivity* refers to how individual members of an organization respond to the information embedded in turbulence to thrive in a turbulence-driven climate.

Welcoming Difference

In the natural world, an event creates turbulence only when it is different from the status quo. The collision of warm, moist air with cool, dry air can create turbulent weather. The intersection of rapidly moving water with still water can produce the turbulence often seen at the delta of a river.

Looking at a business example, let us say the leaders of a computer reseller to Fortune 1000 companies hire a consultant to advise them about what steps they might take to increase their profits. Given the low profit margin on computer goods and the increasing complexity of networking equipment, the consultant suggests that the company promote itself as a networking service provider to large corporations rather than as a retailer—even though it will still also be selling more or less the same retail products it had in the past.

Implementation of this major shift will have tremendous repercussions. The sales and marketing departments will need to alter their focus quite radically. The actual service providers will need to beef up their operations. The legal department will have to come up with new contractual arrangements. This change will have a profound effect on the entire company and, the leaders hope, the company's bottom line.

Now let us say that instead of bringing in a consultant, the executives, after researching sales figures and negotiating with other computer providers, decided to sell one additional product line. The impact of that decision on the organization would be minimal. Part of the sales force would simply change over to selling that new product line, and the sales and marketing departments would include the new products in their promotional materials. Presumably the financial statements would show a similarly negligible change.

The consultant in this example represents the periphery—that place beyond the company's usual area of focus from whence come trends and new ideas. The consultant's recommendations would create a great deal of turbulence. All of the affected departments would need to go into high gear, coming up with new campaigns and new product packages, and employees would be continuously strategizing together and adjusting to the changes as they try to take them to new levels.

A company that practices Positive Turbulence brings new information and new ideas from the periphery inside the organization. Whether those ideas are accepted or rejected depends largely on just how different they are. If the new information is slight or subtle, it will probably go unnoticed. If there is not enough of a difference, the normal surroundings will overcome the turbulence, and the possibilities for stimulation and innovation will be submerged into the background.

Yet if the new information is too different from what is already present, it will be experienced as threatening and disruptive. Overly severe turbulence will summon into action the organizational equivalent of antibodies; the organization's white corpuscles will surround the new information and isolate it—its stimulating potential never perceived as a possible source of vital creativity. In extreme cases, radical difference may bring on a kind of group short-circuit in which the organization is paralyzed. Even worse, the group could be plunged into a downward spiral because, by rejecting the unsettlingly different information, it may also reject vital opportunities for renewal.

Had the consultant instead suggested that the company switch to selling home office equipment to tap into the burgeoning home office market, the change would probably have been too drastic. The company had been dealing almost exclusively with large companies, so, on the one hand, every aspect of the business would need to be completely revamped to adapt to this tumultuous change. On the other hand, not adapting could spell a severe downturn for the company.

Welcoming difference is key to helping a company develop a new focus, create new products, reach new heights. But its leaders must recognize that there are consequences to bringing in difference, and the clue to dealing with it successfully is always being aware of the impact it is having, whether in individual or organizational terms, and being prepared to take corrective measures.

If you are trying something new and it does not seem to be working, maybe it is not different enough, and you need to augment it to make the difference more apparent and more beneficial. If people freeze up and do not know how to respond, it may be because the new ideas are too different, even disruptive. If you open a window and what blows in is not a gentle wind but a hurricane, turning the place upside down, you have allowed in too great a difference and you had better close the window partway.

Inviting Multiple Perspectives

When different ideas are brought into an organization or new information is presented, there could be as many different ways of viewing it as there are individuals looking at it. Then again, there could be just one way—the company way, the way such ideas and information have always been viewed, a way not likely to uncover new directions or new processes needed for renewal. The many ways of viewing the ideas may well lead to renewal because the more possible viewpoints there are, the greater the likelihood is that one will lead to the appropriate interpretation on which people can act in positive new ways.

The reason that multiple perspectives are so critical is that Positive Turbulence depends on making sense of new and different information that by its nature is not fully clear. It is by taking the low-frequency, low-amplitude, static-filled signals from the periphery, examining them from different angles, and interpreting them in fresh ways that we are able to amplify them into something useful. It enables us to see solutions in a different light, act in unanticipated ways, and uncover new possibilities.

Seeing Anew

Much like the prophets of times past found on the periphery of society, artists today provide society with the ability to look at something from new perspectives. They help us shift our centric, parochial focus to the fringes. They illuminate what has just entered—or foretell what is about to enter—from the peripheries of our society and our culture.

The organizational equivalent of the artist's role is the people who, by training or natural inclination, see their environment slightly differently from the rest of us. In large organizations this role may fall to the strategic planner, but it could just as well be a person who simply enjoys thinking off the beat. Both of them provide interpretations of the distant trends or early warnings that signal that change is needed and in which direction the change must go.

Common to any enlightened process for interpreting information is the perspective that people, and the organizations they represent, are held prisoner by single-frame, heads-down thinking, and that this orientation limits their ability to respond to problems or indicators of change in novel and creative ways. When multiple perspectives are considered, multiple frames of reference are produced, and these provide several alternative ways to respond to new information, none of which would have been apparent when seen through the old framework. The narrowly focused manner of thinking does, however, have a place: helping an organization maintain quality, efficiency, and profitability.

Acting in Fresh Ways

Seeing and thinking are usually the prelude to taking action. Once vision and thoughts are broadened, the options for action increase dramatically. The more perspectives there are, the more possibilities the management team has for finding the most promising course of action.

By shifting the definition of the problem, changing the problem's context, or asking new questions, new courses of action unfold, sometimes even spontaneously. Even something so simple as seeing with an unfettered perspective an inanimate object having unusual properties can trigger an entirely new way of doing things. Consider what happened to Charles Kettering (1992) while window shopping at Tiffany & Co.

Kettering, the newly appointed head of research for General Motors, had been wrestling with the problem of reducing the time required to paint new cars—or, more specifically, reducing the time it took the paint to dry. Newly painted cars were moved into storage areas for several days and allowed to air dry slowly—an expensive use of space and a production bottleneck. The engineers had told Kettering that there was no way to speed up the drying process.

One afternoon as he was strolling down Fifth Avenue in Manhattan, Kettering stopped to look at a beautiful vase in a Tiffany's window. Admiring its lustrous shine, he wondered about the lacquer used on it. That started him on a trail that eventually led to a garage in New Jersey, where a lone artist was applying the wondrous lacquer to other pieces. No, the man said; he did not think his lacquer would work in GM's spray guns, because it dried too fast and would blow away before it reached the car bodies. The GM engineers had told Kettering there was no way the drying process could be speeded up, and the lacquer maker was telling him there was no way the process could be slowed down!

But Kettering persevered, and eventually a new formula for paint was developed that dried in one hour rather than several days. The reexamination of the problem in a completely uncharacteristic way had been stimulated by a process used in a totally different context. It provided the automobile industry with a very timely and important process for the mass production of automobiles.

Opening New Possibilities

The result of looking at a problem from an unexpected viewpoint is not always so dramatic, the problem not always so clear-cut. Population trends give us one big example of a less-than-clear circumstance. We all know that the world's population is increasing, but the change is gradual and thus easy to overlook. But by the year 2001, says Peter Schwartz (1991), there will be more than 2 billion teenagers in the world. According to William Taylor (1997), by the year 2010 it is estimated that there will be five million Americans one hundred years or older—a thousand-fold increase from 1960. Without an obvious crisis to force action, how can organizations take the fact of population trends and find useful strategic information therein? Examining the situation from multiple perspectives provides the answer.

Skandia, Sweden's $7 billion 140-year-old insurance giant, has done just that (LaBarre, 1997). It created a strategic planning unit, the Skandia Futures Centers, staffed with people having diverse organizational experiences and different cultural backgrounds who range in age from their mid-twenties to their mid-sixties. Skandia commonly refers to it as the 3G (generational) future planning team, because it is purposefully constructed with equal numbers from each generation.

Leif Edvinsson, the person responsible for Skandia's planning process, seeks to include people who are often disenfranchised—the young or less experienced. "We need people who understand the archeology of the future," he said. "That's why we have these 25-year-olds. They carry the icons of tomorrow with them."

The very fact of the generational differences sparks a number of interesting dialogues within the group—discussions on medical realities such as dying, the slowing of the aging process, the end of disease, and the impact of these changes on the younger generations.

All of these trends (and perhaps realities) have implications for actuarial decisions, future selling strategies, products, market niche decisions, and even qualification procedures for future customers. That is why it is important to have a generationally diverse group examining them.

Inviting multiple perspectives is a central part of organizational change. It is the way that forward-thinking leaders can gently coax (or violently wrench, if that is what is needed) their organization out of its traditional perspective. The sparks that come about when old frameworks scrape against new perspectives ignite creativity.

Controlling the Intensity of Turbulence

Turbulence can be an intense force. At its most extreme it can cause upheaval and disruption. At its weakest it can cause slight flutters. When it leads to disarray and destruction, it is Negative Turbulence, and when it stimulates growth and renewal, it is Positive Turbulence.

To understand the full impact of Negative Turbulence, we have only to think of the devastation visited on corporations in recent years through downsizing, sometimes called that absurd euphemism *rightsizing*. The soul-wrenching tumult felt throughout the organization, by survivors as well as those downsized, is the keenest example of an atmosphere so chaotic that everyone in it is rendered ineffective. Moreover, downsizing has not always achieved its goals—either financial or organizational. And no one should be surprised at the profound negative effect it has on motivation, productivity, and individual creativity.

There may be some downsizing survivors who feel positively about the changes that have taken place in their organizations, but I have not talked to a single employee who believes that his or her situation has improved because of the downsizing. This view is supported by research conducted by Teresa Amabile, professor of business administration at Harvard University, and Regina Conti, assistant professor of psychology at Colgate University (1995), suggesting that the greatest cost to an organization as a result of downsizing is the erosion of employee trust and commitment. When employees no longer trust, they are often less willing to put in extra hours or effort. Because workers feel disempowered, they are less willing to risk bringing in new ideas from the peripheries.

That same research revealed that traditional creativity indicators also suggested a decline. The average number of patent applications decreased by 12 percent and invention disclosures declined by 24 percent following the downsizing that Amabile and Conti tracked. They discovered that employees who remained were less open to new ideas because they perceived anything that was new as being dangerous. Speed and efficiency of information exchange deteriorated to the point that communication was almost nonexistent.

Downsizing clearly generated Negative Turbulence. Although the changes brought into the downsized organizations were indeed new and novel, they were not the kind necessary for creativity. Because they were not controlled and properly managed, they tipped the ongoing organizational processes off balance and led to chaos and dysfunction.

Whenever new information and different ideas (think of the consultant's recommendation to the computer company) are brought into the corporation and multiple perspectives are sought, things naturally are stirred up. Key to keeping the turbulence in the positive zone is being able to control the speed and magnitude of the turbulence while maintaining a viable business.

On the one hand, trying to deal with new information that is coming in too fast and in too great a volume is like trying to get a drink of water by putting a fire hose in your mouth; you cannot help but be fully overwhelmed. For the organization, a too-fast and too-dense flow of information would create such a high level of turbulence that the organization would have to take a self-protective stance, and the new information would never be integrated into the current operating system.

On the other hand, information that comes in too slowly is like the slow drip of an IV solution, and also has negative results: the new information passes by completely unnoticed or is folded into the status quo. The organization would never experience the stimulation that comes with turbulence, and opportunities for innovation are lost.

It is worth pointing out that the concept of speed is closely linked to the concept of volume; both have the same ability to overwhelm. I experienced this fire-hose-in-the-mouth overload of information not long ago when I attended COMDEX, a computer trade show extravaganza. I went because I wanted to see what cutting-edge technology was available that could provide the Center for Creative Leadership with the means to remain current with our clients and effective in the classroom.

Mind numbing in size and dazzle, the 1997 show featured 2,100 exhibitors and more than 220,000 visitors. Even industry veterans felt overwhelmed, not to mention outsiders such as myself, but I was determined not to miss out on the worthwhile ideas.

I discovered a useful way to deal with this particular fire hose: I asked a knowledgeable colleague to guide me through the maze. We began by my listing the problems I wanted to solve and the questions I wanted answered. My guide then turned to the schedule of events, which lists the exhibitors in relevant categories, and suggested the booths that were most likely to have the relevant software and hardware. And she said, "Oh, by the way, I saw a demonstration of CD-ROM-based training at the Intel exhibit that works for us. Perhaps CCL can use it too." Then we went straight to the five exhibits that would be most meaningful to me, bypassing all the rest.

Filtering out the irrelevant from a large volume of information has the same effect as slowing a fast rate of speed: it allows people to make sense out of what could otherwise knock them flat.

Not uncommonly, a blur of new information exhibits both excessive speed *and* excessive degree of difference. The organization's leaders then will need an approach for managing the turbulence level. Returning again to the computer company, let us suppose that managers bring back reports of the consultant's findings to their departments. They announce that the company has been operating in the red for too many months and the only solution is for the company to focus solely on the market for home offices.

You can well imagine the turmoil that would be set in motion as a consequence and the number of employees who, fearing layoffs, would abandon ship, as well as the dispirited, demoralized atmosphere that would prevail in the company. If indeed home office products were the way to go, the company's leaders would have presented their case with much greater success if they had controlled the rate at which they released information and implemented the changeover more gradually, at each stage reassuring employees about what they were doing and why.

Employees at Texaco Inc. (see Figure 2.1) experienced severe overloads of information before the company implemented means for managing its release. According to John Old, the company's director of Knowledge Management, Texaco sought to resolve these volume and speed issues in a number of ways using special software systems. First, the company introduced software agents to customize the information received based on parameters an individual employee might set. Second, it has developed repositories of information that employees can access when they are ready, rather than having to respond to a blast from some information zealot. Third, the company provides visuals (color graphs and charts) of the information that allow individuals to filter and process more information than they might through just reading words.

Once the amount of information any person can pay attention to gets to a certain level, the circuits seem to short out. The person stops paying attention altogether, overreacts, or does not react at all. This response creates even more noise (or volume) in the system, and thus begins a vicious cycle that Texaco is trying to stop.

Developing Receptivity

Business leaders can impose a reorganization on a company. They can impose a dress code. They can also impose Positive Turbulence, but unless they have taken care to develop receptivity to this process, it runs the risk of failure. If employees do not learn to value and use Positive Turbulence, all that energy will just dissipate or, worse, cause disarray.

Receptivity to anything is in large degree a function of one's sensitivities and sensibilities, so the different styles that individuals have impinge on how they adapt to and work with Positive Turbulence. People may differ in their style of defining a problem and finding creative solutions to it, in their reaction to uncertainty and ambiguity—some are motivated to reduce ambiguity, while others tolerate and even enjoy entertaining it—and in their ways of thinking—whether they take a linear or nonlinear approach.

Sensitivities and sensibilities, personality and proclivities, are factors that can affect receptivity to Positive Turbulence. It is important to value differences for effective utilization of the knowledge coming in from the periphery while maintaining ongoing operations.

Figure 2.1. Texaco's System for Organizing Information from the Periphery

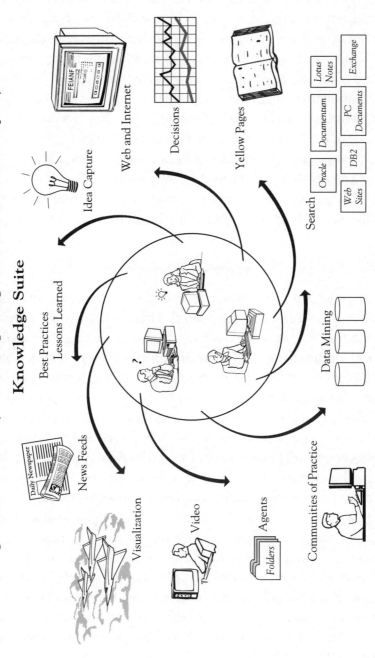

Knowledge Suite

Idea Capture

Web and Internet

Decisions

Yellow Pages

Search

Oracle   Documentum   Lotus Notes

Web Sites   DB2   PC Documents   Exchange

Best Practices
Lessons Learned

Data Mining

News Feeds

Visualization

Video

Agents

Folders

Communities of Practice

Finding Appropriate Problem-Solving Styles

Positive Turbulence includes capturing new information and ideas and using them to find creative solutions to different problems. How people resolve the problems often has to do with their problem-solving style. The goal of an astute manager in a Positive Turbulence–driven organization is to match the problem-solving style of the person to the problem at hand to produce the most effective solution.

People generally fall into one of two categories: some accept the problem as it is defined; others redefine it. Michael J. Kirton (1976, 1989) has defined the former as adaptors and the latter as innovators. Adaptors are more likely to use the turbulence in the system for producing a creative response described as better or resourceful—ideas that stay within the accepted definition of the problem. Innovators, by rejecting problem definitions they confront, are more likely to use the turbulence for producing an original response that goes outside the problem as first defined and results in an idea described as different.

Thus the same turbulence can result in quite different solutions—resourceful or original—depending on the creativity style (adaptive or innovative) of the person making the connection between the turbulence and the need or problem. Both styles are necessary in an organization because some problems require adaptive solutions and others require wholly new ones.

Consider the company that produced the glass beads known as cats' eyes that reflect car headlights along roads so that drivers can better see the lane demarcations at night. The company had accumulated a small mountain of these because road construction had slowed. The problem then became what to do with the beads and how the company could continue to exist if its products were no longer needed.

The adaptor approach was to convince the transportation authorities to line the sides of roads with the reflectors, which would require a twofold increase in glass beads needed. The innovator approach was to change the formula for the glass so that a liquid placed inside a hollow glass bead—say, an herbicide or a medication—could permeate the glass walls in a controlled, time-released manner. The first solution is immediately implementable yet has limitations; there are still only so many highways requiring cats' eyes. The second is a dramatic new concept with perhaps unlimited use, yet it requires time for the technology to be tested, for the Food and Drug Administration to approve it, and for the marketplace to accept it.

When I was called into Goodyear, a serious problem was put in the hands of people with the wrong problem-solving style. This took place in the late 1970s and the early 1980s, when the French tire manufacturer Michelin introduced the radial tire to American consumers, and Goodyear's market share dropped.

Although the U.S. tire company had been watching the French radials take a whopping 40 percent bite out of the European market, it waited to respond (a perfect example of not using the information coming in from the periphery). When it finally introduced bias-belted tires that could be produced on the old machines, this was only a stopgap measure.

The leadership at Goodyear set up a system to collect creative ideas for responding to this threat. It established innovation committees at four levels. After four levels of screening, the best ideas were sent to the chairman, who rejected every last one of them as not being creative enough.

Without getting into too many details, I can say that I identified the fourth level of screening as being largely responsible for the rejection of the innovatively creative solutions submitted. The positions and problem-solving styles of the employees in the fourth level (all country managers with twenty-five years of experience who had made their mark by making a better, more cost-effective tire the old-fashioned way) were not what Goodyear needed to screen new ideas. François Michelin had changed the rules of the game, and these employees were not able to play to win.

More significant for our purposes here, all members of the fourth-level committee had the same problem-solving style, and it was the inappropriate one: they accepted the problem as defined, without questioning its parameters. And so they offered suggestions that would improve their current product. The kind of thinking that Goodyear needed at this time of crisis was the nontraditional kind that would produce an idea along the caliber of the radial tire. The only way to get truly original solutions to a problem—the innovator approach that was required here—is first to ask whether the problem is correctly defined given the content and redefine it as necessary.

I concluded that the chairman would have gotten a more effective response if two quite distinct activities had taken place: (1) the chairman had been more specific with his request for innovatively creative ideas, and (2) the members of the fourth-level committee recognized their own preferred style of problem definition and were able to implement new behavior. It is not always comfortable to take on a new style, but in a critical situation it may be necessary. Without the ability to do so, the winds of Positive Turbulence can drive a company into the ground.

My suggestion was that the fourth-level screening committee resurrect the ideas it had rejected as being too outrageous. For example, one idea was for a mothballed ship, an aircraft carrier, to be fitted out and turned into a state-of-the-art tire manufacturing facility. When we reconsidered this proposal, we discovered that similar floating facilities actually existed— papermaking plants in Latin America that float along rivers. With the chairman giving a clear mandate— "I want creative ideas that are truly different"—these outrageous ideas now made sense and were more likely to be considered and accepted.

Fostering Tolerance of Ambiguity

Some people become irritated or anxious when they find themselves in conditions of uncertainty and cannot anticipate likely outcomes or understand exactly what is driving the situation. Others manage uncertainty by ignoring it. Some people derive the greater satisfaction in discovering the nature of uncertainty and perceive its resolution as pleasant. This suggests that the best course is to develop a stance of entertaining ambiguity. This choice increases the possibility that the new and different information coming in from the periphery will be tolerated, then understood, processed, and used in a meaningful way.

Ambiguity is a state in which many possibilities exist. To make an analogy, when the artist faces a completely blank canvas, there are literally millions of pictures that could be created. It has been said that the first stroke of the artist's brush destroys countless numbers of possible paintings, and each successive dab of paint limits the number of paintings that are possible on that canvas even more.

Complete ambiguity is, practically speaking, the same as chaos, and all of us can become nervous in total chaos, so we all have an urge to impose order. Some of us move quickly to close boundaries and contain ambiguity. Others prefer to entertain ambiguity or at least some element of it; they are in less of a rush to nail everything down, and they like to leave a little wiggle room in the product or process they are creating. These are the people who are seen as most successfully creative. People who can delay closure can find more uses for turbulence, beyond the immediate.

OshKosh B'Gosh, the clothing manufacturer, cited in J. Dru's book, *Disruption* (1996), was able to work with ambiguity when it decided to change its product line when demand for adult overalls was slowing. At around the same time, the company looked at market data showing an increasing need for hard-wearing clothes for children. The company that knew everything there was to know about overalls for adults decided to adapt and apply that knowledge to overalls for children.

Today children's clothing represents more than 95 percent of OshKosh's sales—a successful transformation that depended on the company's ability to tolerate and not reject a brand-new self-image, at the same time exploiting a market opportunity.

Encouraging Nonlinear Thinking

Many of us, by temperament and training, find it easier and more practical to think and speak in controlled, concise terms. We stay on the subject at hand, with one idea following closely after the other in an orderly manner. This style of thinking has been called linear. Others, again by personal disposition or by training, have learned that there are advantages to occasionally departing from that style of thinking. They have been known to unleash their thoughts to range about like hunting dogs in a wide-open field. Their thinking is called nonlinear, and it is this style that has been cited in research as being characteristic of people who are often successful in creative problem solving.

It is easy to illustrate the notion of nonlinear thinking with a simple word association test. Ask a friend to name the first thing that flashes into her mind when you say "fast food." Your friend will probably respond with "junk food, frozen food, hamburgers, fried chicken." Those are close associations. Then ask her to think of additional examples quickly. Now she has to move beyond the conventional first associations and top-of-the-head ideas and range into other categories. She may jump to a category of "convenient foods," which require little preparation, like raw vegetables and fresh fruit, or items that are quickly digested, like fruit juice or hot soup. At that point, most people will stop thinking about fast food because they have already provided an abundance of appropriate examples.

People who have been trained in a form of nonlinear thinking known as remote association or who have an apparently inborn tendency to keep on associating to a cue concept will broaden the cognitive search and come up with other, less closely associated ideas. They might mention airline food, trout, deer, or partridges (food that itself often moves swiftly)—or green apples and stewed prunes (foods that move through our digestive system quickly).

The more different ideas we process, the more likely it is that other associations not at all closely related to the original topic will be triggered. When ordinary reasoning is required, remote associating is counterproductive, so most of us have learned to shut down our idea association machinery when it threatens to run too far away from the starting point.

In a serious business setting, linear reasoning is the norm. However, when we are trying to get a new handle on some problem or to think of ways to improve or to change a process, shutting down thinking quickly can interfere with employing our best capacities. There is usually time and opportunity to get logical about a speculative idea, to tame and harness it to some practical application. But if we always stay too close to linear thinking, we may not surface that one good idea. We trap ourselves without even knowing we are doing it.

Whether a person possesses the mental receptors that permit nonlinear thinking and remote association is directly linked to how well that person will be able to connect turbulence to a potential application in the organization. A person who freely makes remote associations can gain greater benefit from the surrounding turbulence than a person who does not; in the second person, the same new information will result in a narrower range of ideas with quite limited possibilities.

In looking at the dynamics of Positive Turbulence—what drives it and how it drives an organization—we have seen that by understanding the four critical aspects of Positive Turbulence—difference, multiple perspectives, intensity, and receptivity—leaders ensure that the turbulence they experience does not have negative repercussions but remains a positive force for innovation and renewal.

We have also seen that although each of these aspects is essential, receptivity is really the sine qua non, because without creating a climate willing to accept Positive Turbulence, you'll be blowing in the wind.

Chapter Three

Strategies for Increasing Receptivity to Positive Turbulence

Positive Turbulence is not an easy concept for employees to grasp and adapt to because it often involves seeing and thinking in unfamiliar ways. That is why encouraging them to think and see differently deepens their ability to understand and benefit from Positive Turbulence. When employees broaden their knowledge and experiences (of other disciplines, other areas in the company, and other parts of the world) and have ample opportunities for reinvigoration, they come to value difference, appreciate intensity, and open up to fresh approaches. Positive Turbulence can thrive in this environment, and continuous renewal finds its stride.

Broadening Knowledge and Experiences

Positive Turbulence involves taking in, processing, and working with information and ideas that may come from all different sources and relate to all kinds of different topics. A person who is used to handling only one kind of information from one source may find the new information unmanageable. Similarly, an employee who keeps to a narrow track, rarely experiencing anything other than the usual, and is then put in an entirely new situation, may be unable to function.

The antidote to this kind of debilitation is providing opportunities for learning how to integrate new information and then offering a variety of integration experiences. This training helps to ensure an openness and a receptivity to the wealth of new information and situations that arrive frequently and often unpredictably in an organization driven by Positive Turbulence. Learning about other disciplines, other countries, and even other areas in the company provides a good basis for broadening knowledge and experiences. The personal broadening helps the individual turn turbulence into a positive experience.

Other Fields

As we saw in the previous chapter, solutions to seemingly insoluble problems often come from far afield. Charles Kettering at GM used Tiffany's lacquered vase to find a way to speed up his automotive production. Presumably Kettering would have never thought to research vase painting to help find ways to resolve the paint drying dilemma. But the very fact of exploring other fields can identify new frames of reference, new pools of information. And even if none of this is directly applicable, sometimes the very process of learning about different fields catalyzes a new way of thinking or of looking at a problem down the line.

Nissan Design International (NDI), a design center for Nissan Motor Corporation, encourages employees to develop secondary areas of interest and regularly take a break to do so. "Just as we can extend aerobic activity by using different muscles, we can extend and enhance our powers of focus and creativity by shifting mental gears," says Jerry Hirshberg (1998), founding director of NDI, who refers to this experience as "drinking from diverse wells." He explains it as the "intermixing of broad, generalized experience with focused, honed skills, [which] dramatically heightens the prospects for the kind of thinking that elicits aha reactions."

Some of this outside experience has resulted in NDI's design of speedboats, children's furniture, golf clubs, and even vacuum cleaners. "Sensitivities and skills gained from having worked with forms of this [breadth and] magnitude gave NDI some unique advantages over most car design studios limiting themselves to working on only one product and at one scale," says Hirshberg.

Because NDI also contracts out its design expertise, employees get to "drink from diverse wells" at the same time they are working for the company. And often experience gained outside the usual field has a direct application to the regular work. That was the case with a boat design that sparked rethinking interior car design.

Hospitals provide another example. Some CEOs of these hospitals are having management employees learn about how hotels are run. If patients are seen as customers, they reason, then hospitals could well learn how to make their entranceways and waiting rooms look and seem more like grand hotels so "guests" feel more comfortable and heal faster.

We broaden our knowledge and experience of other fields by reading about them, attending conferences outside our area of expertise, and joining professional networks outside the organization.

Reading Outside Your Field. Some twenty years ago, Conrad Kasperson (1978), professor of business administration at Franklin and Marshall College, studied information-receiving behaviors, comparing, in particular, the information flow around creative and noncreative scientists. He found that the scientists who were encouraged to read outside their disciplines (and given time to do so) and were allowed to attend conferences that only tangentially related to their field of expertise were the more creative ones. In the years since then, I have often observed that these two practices are common denominators in creative organizations of all types.

Kasperson's research demonstrates a correlation between scientific creativity and channels of information that clearly supports the basic tenet of Positive Turbulence: when information impulses from the periphery are allowed to penetrate the company core and stir up the thinking mode of its people, innovative solutions arise. These new channels of information, Kasperson found, provide individual scientists with opportunities for reframing their ideas or having their ideas scrape against the current thinking of the day.

To translate Kasperson's research into practical applications in today's organizations, I suggest deliberately expanding the range of books and periodicals you read regularly as well as Web sites that you follow. Include some from completely different fields, and find one or two that are clearly on the fringe of current thinking.

If, for example, you work in the retail industry and you read material generally thought to be for the technology industry, you could learn, for example, about wearable computers with head-mounted monitors small enough to be projected onto eyeglasses (Marriot, 1998). This miniature computer allows inventory control staff to roam storerooms and store aisles, entering and accessing information and responding accordingly. If you are in the building industry, you might want to read literature geared toward senior citizens to gain understanding into their housing needs. As you read, do not rush to make connections; rather, let the information seep in and percolate.

At the Center for Creative Leadership, we have learned a great deal about creativity and how it can be applied to businesses from a jazz musician, Bobby Bradford (1983). Through him we have learned about the need to practice what he calls "the discipline of improvisation." Jazz musicians must be creative every night—in Bradford's words, "Every night we must come out and dance on a slippery floor." But the conditions are always different—a new audience, a different group of musicians, changed mood. The musicians must learn how to adapt to those different conditions on the spot and come up with exciting, creative music. Corporate managers too face constantly changing business environments, to which they must also learn to adapt through improvisation. By paying attention to the indicators and direction of change, as jazz musicians must do, they can make the necessary adjustments within their organizations.

We also learned from Bradford about looking to the future for new trends while being supported by the strength of the past. According to Bradford, significant changes in jazz occurred when newcomers in the field, like Charlie Parker in the 1950s, standing on the shoulders of giants like Louis Armstrong, were able to look on the other side of the wall and play what they were then able to envision as the future form of jazz.

Bradford also had a lot to say about teams, because a jazz combo is, after all, a small group. Members who are good and exhibit the diverse skills needed on the team must be allowed to come to the fore and make their own personal contribution when appropriate. Members are not on the team to make the leader look good. Leaders, then, should pick the most talented individuals for their team and then let their skills act in synergy. In Chapter Four, when we look at teams, we will see how applicable his ideas are to teams in business organizations.

Another way to expand your horizons through reading outside your field is to study the history of change in other fields, looking for parallel events that can be used to predict relevant change in your own field. In this way, you can be on top of the changes before they occur, and they will be less of a surprise to your project or to your organization.

Appendix A lists what I call credible fringe business publications along with their addresses and brief descriptions. These publications—*Fast Company*, *Wired*, *Leadership in Action*, *Red Herring*, *Upside*, and *@Issue: The Journal of Business and Design*, among others—have yet to become mainstream, but they are credible enough for readers seeking surges of Positive Turbulence to find in them ideas of value that in time will become accepted as mainstream or conventional, or considered as viable, sound alternatives. Although you may not read these periodicals or even have heard of many of them, you should realize that periodicals such as *Business Week*, *Fortune*, the *Economist*, *U.S. News and World Report*, and even the *Wall Street Journal* and the *Financial Times of London* were by definition probably not mainstream when they first appeared. Yet today they are, and they are regarded as fundamental sources for information about business.

Perhaps if you pick up this book ten years after its publication date, some of these fringe periodicals will have moved onto center stage and become recognized as part of the new establishment. Others will undoubtedly have failed or moved off the list, and others moved in.

My list is a suggestion only; it focuses on publications about business because that is the world in which I live and work, and also because overall business and economic trends are significant for all industries. I suggest that you develop a list of credible fringe periodicals that depict the signs of change within your own field or industry—those that challenge the established way. Read these for sources of novelty of perspective and possible application. Remember that today's established ideas were once fringe and even radical before they were accepted and became mainstream. So it is with the periodicals.

Attending Conferences Outside Your Field. Kasperson's second observation (1978) about the more creative R&D scientists was that they took the time to attend conferences dealing with topics outside their field. I heartily recommend it, and not just for scientists. In fact, I suggest a simple formula for line managers and human resource or training directors to consider when making decisions about spending training and travel dollars. The implementation of this formula will test the organization's readiness to invest in Positive Turbulence.

The formula is: $N + 1$, with N representing the number of professional meetings you or your people attend each year. It is my experience that attending such meetings is contingent on the conference theme's relating directly to the professional's field of expertise or the role she or he plays inside that sponsoring professional organization. Since I am a psychologist interested in creativity in organizations, I can more easily request and receive travel dollars (or defend budget line items) that include conferences sponsored by such organizations as the American Psychological Association, the Academy of Management, the Creative Education Foundation, and the American Society for Training and Development.

Let some combination of these four organizations' conferences equal N. What I have to solve for each year is 1—the one additional conference I should attend that provides me with the different perspective I need for my own personal and professional growth.

We are experts to varying degrees in our own profession or field of experience. What we need to kick-start our receptivity to Positive Turbulence is some novel stimulation to jostle the known perspective and ideas we have from our own profession. In both your reading and your conference attendance, look for surprises. Avoid thinking that the idea you produce or the connection you make must be fallible because someone else surely would think of it if it is not. That is usually not the case. Be sure to see your idea through to conclusion; it may be a winner.

Recall my experience at COMDEX in the hands of a savvy guide. The COMDEX show is designed for those in some facet of the computer industry, and some might think that I had no business at all there. But since advances in technology affect every industry and every organization, it behooves all of us to familiarize ourselves with what lies down the road. Some of the ideas I came away with from COMDEX include CD-ROM-based assessments and Web-based leadership training.

Not long after the COMDEX show I observed a demonstration of virtual surgery, whereby a neurosurgeon in London directed a particular surgery in which he specialized, on a patient in Los Angeles. As I watched the delicate operation it suddenly occurred to me that the same technology that made the virtual surgery possible could greatly improve our ability to deliver distance learning. We could, for example, have classroom trainers in a television studio and the trainees dispersed all over the world and hooked up by satellite. There could be frequent interactive exercises, and the "talking-head" time could be limited, so trainees, though separated by many miles, could still experience engagement with the process.

If I am to help my organization provide better ideas for serving our customers, it is important for me to know about and engage the possibilities. This training possibility indirectly led to a second-place award for Best Distance Learning Series—Continuing Education category at the Sixteenth Annual TeleCon Academy Awards of Teleconferencing for a trainer from the Center for Creative Leadership.

Seeing something in one field and getting an idea how to apply it to another is the point in attending conferences outside one's field. And the only way to make these cross-connections is to put yourself in the thick of things. Among the most dazzling experiences I have had in this regard is the conference entitled TED (Technology Entertainment Design), which takes place in Monterey, California, under the guidance of Richard Saul Wurman. *Communication Arts* (Coyne, 1994) described one TED as "an opportunity to hear the opinions of many notable visionaries on the possible future of communications." I was introduced to this amazing event by Hallmark staffers, who attend regularly, and I found it an intellectually festive party of unequaled Positive Turbulence. (For some, it may border on overexuberant turbulence at too fast a rate of speed.)

Available in one setting for my creative pleasure were John Perry Barlow (cofounder of Electronic Frontier Foundation, lyricist for the Grateful Dead), Ben Cohen (chair of Ben & Jerry's Homemade), Larry Ellison (chair and CEO of Oracle Corporation), Jim Fowler (naturalist and author), Bill Gates (founder of Microsoft), Frank Gehry (architect), Matt Golombek (Mars Pathfinder Project scientist), Stephen Jay Gould (biologist), Herbie Hancock (jazz musician), Jaron Lanier (pioneer in virtual reality), Geraldine Laybourne (creator of Nickelodeon), Jane Metcalfe (cofounder of *Wired* magazine), Paul Saffo (of the Institute for the Future), Jonas Salk (scientist, humanitarian, developer of the polio vaccine), Forrest Sawyer (correspondent for *Nightline*, ABC News), Oliver Stone (film producer and director), John Walsh (director of the J. P. Getty Museum), and Jerry Yang (cofounder of Yahoo!). They were matched by the challenging list of attendees from companies such as Apple Computer, Hanna Barbera, U S WEST Communication Group, Microsoft, Herman Miller, the Museum of Modern Art, General Magic, Prince, Viacom, Time-Life Books, Intel, Novartis AG, and Nike.

By acknowledging the value of attending conferences outside an employee's usual field, managers underscore the importance of using outside information and experiences to catalyze internal changes. By helping their employees become more receptive to Positive Turbulence through attending conferences, they ensure that these people will promote the goals of Positive Turbulence and increase receptivity to it among other employees.

Joining Professional External Networks. Becoming a member of a professional network is another way to broaden one's knowledge and experiences and hence one's receptivity to Positive Turbulence. External networks often bring together individuals from different companies and different fields who share insights (and frustrations) in an open, supportive environment. They offer the opportunity to learn different ways to solve common problems, interpret different issues. Because they are not bound to the "what's in it for me" framework forced on us by the more typical organizational norms, networks allow for a great deal of creative thinking and problem resolution, usually done in a collaborative spirit.

Let us say you are a member of a regional Women in Marketing network. There may be women in it from publishing, technology, manufacturing, and retail. How a woman from a local publishing company deals with the daily newspaper will likely be very different from the way a woman from a manufacturing company might. Through strategizing together about how to boost their visibility, for example, they may share ideas that come from their unique perspectives yet are very helpful to someone coming from a very different perspective.

I belong to AMI, the Association for Managers of Innovation, a network that has been in existence since 1981. Its sole purpose is to function as a learning network for members who manage the innovation process within their own company. Proprietary information stays outside the meeting's door, and the agenda revolves around three process dynamics.

We ask members who attend to come to each meeting with a Brag, a Beg, and a What-If. (A Brag: "We have been able to speed up the products in our R&D pipeline significantly by redefining our stage gate criteria in this manner." A Beg: "Our president wants a cutting-edge presenter on the topic of innovation. Have you had any experience with the following three experts . . .? Are their presentation styles engaging?" A What-If: "What if leaders were taught about creativity at an earlier age? Could we influence future leaders by having scouting (boys and girls) accept a merit badge on creativity and innovation?") This framing of the agenda has guaranteed the longevity of this group of fifty, with a solid core of fifteen members who have been part of the group for more than eight years. We have invited poets, musicians, furniture designers, photographers, science-fiction writers, and actors to help us think and see in new ways, which opens us up to new possibilities and allows the Positive Turbulence within our own organizations to resonate within us in productive ways.

One intriguing variation on this theme is that of internal networks—a collaboration of organizational members who get together formally or informally to share ideas and brainstorm solutions to identified problems. DuPont's Industrial Fibers Technical Division (Tanner, 1997) started such an internal network. Known as the Oz Creative Thinking Network, it is a volunteer group of DuPont employees who want to learn more about the field of creativity and successful innovation in industry.

It functions somewhat like a support group for highly creative people within this one organization, so members feel that they are not alone. The group is given assignments that bring the collective creativity of its members to bear on current problems within DuPont that could benefit from a creative solution. For example, the Oz network rescued a $30 million project from termination by initiating a creative thinking session that led to a successful plan of action. The perceived barriers were overcome and the project put back on track by the combined efforts of this internal affinity group.

The internal Oz network grew from 7 to more than 750 members in just ten years, and its membership represents most of DuPont's business units. Meetings allow members to interact with internal (and external) experts who address current issues the Oz membership has identified as being of importance within the company.

Not only does this network generate turbulence by bringing in outside speakers and originating innovative solutions, but it exposes other employees to the new ideas and problem-solving modes they come up with as a consequence of membership, and so helps to enhance receptivity to Positive Turbulence companywide.

Networks serve individuals and their organizations with sources of information. We cannot know everything, and networks serve to link us with those who have information we may lack. They force us outside of what we already know.

Other Countries

I do not think any other single activity does more for widening any-one's vision than travel. Those of you who traveled or lived abroad as students will recall the constant reevaluation and reinterpreta-tion you did to survive intellectually as a student. Recall the end-less arguments over coffee trying to explain, then justify, your own values and the culture in which they were embedded. What won-derful turbulence—the kind that causes personal stretching, test-ing, and awareness building, all important by-products of travel.

Encouraging Travel. This cultural and creative enrichment is no less valuable when we become adults; if anything, it is more so, for the benefit accrues not only to our own minds and hearts but also to the collective creative energy of the organizations where we spend our working hours. Enlightened companies know this, take a more active organizational stance, and encourage their employ-ees to take advantage of travel experiences. Some even provide them. Growth, personal and professional, will most likely take place when new worlds are being explored. The sooner and the longer the travel is, the more likely it is that a strong developmen-tal event will take place.

Roger Milliken of Milliken & Company, a large textile company, believes strongly in the benefit of travel. He has been known to charter a jet for a large number of his company's development staff to attend a textile manufacturing equipment trade show outside the United States. He also rented a hotel conference room so that the entire group could begin the day having breakfast together and end it having dinner with one another. At these meals they discussed their assignments for the day and came back with ideas for applying new machinery they saw.

Promoting Foreign Assignments. Closely related to the idea of travel is the deliberate strategy of assigning key people to positions in overseas offices. With nearly every industry targeting fast-growing foreign markets, more companies are requiring foreign work experience for top management positions. Employees who work and live abroad return to their offices in the United States with new understandings that apply not just to working with foreign companies but with their own coworkers.

AMP Incorporated, for example, the world's leading supplier of electrical and electronic connectors, began an extensive program to develop "globe-able leaders" by giving managers international exposure. The company implemented a strategic expatriate assignment program with the sole purpose of developing managers to master global business skills, internalize key globalization concepts, and be able to function effectively anywhere in the world. The ultimate purpose was for AMP to remain a leader within the global marketplace.

Other Areas in the Company

Very often within a corporate environment we become so entrenched in our own departments that we fail to see the forest for the trees. The more narrow our thinking is, the more unwilling we often are to entertain other styles, other modalities, other perspectives. When a strong gust of turbulence comes in from anywhere—another department, the executive branch, the strategic planner—we are unprepared. One way companies have found to decrease the possibility of this happening is by moving employees into different roles and bringing into a company someone who has come from a completely different background.

Promoting Role Changes.   Companies that use role changes experimentally move people outside their well-learned roles and across silos into new functional positions. The introduction of uncertainty and new perspectives and a new sense of a need to communicate with each other often results in novel exchanges that can lead to creating new ideas. We now have the local knowledge of one function moving over into another, yet within the same company.

In the glory days of Bendix Corporation, it was not unheard of to find the treasurer being moved into the position of vice president of human resources. New perspectives were then brought to a particular role, and all perspectives and skills were shared at the senior level. The multitude of perspectives provided for a knowledgeable senior team with regard to strategy implementation and permanent renewal.

To get an idea of the kind of shake-up in thinking that can result from changing roles, consider what happens at some Disney resorts, where children take their grandparents into what I call a reverse petting zoo. There the adults, guided and instructed by the children, can see and touch a mouse—an "electronic mouse." The children experience the role of teacher, and the adults get an introduction to the computer world.

Some companies, like Norfolk Southern, which we look at closely in Chapter Six, provide all sorts of ways that employees can explore new roles in other parts of the company. They bring their familiar knowledge and experiences with them, combine that background with the new position and its responsibilities, and often come up with entirely new ways of seeing and doing things.

These kinds of role changes are usually decreed by the company itself. A senior-level manager with vision decides to shake up the mixture, to reenergize what may have become stagnant. Intelligent, motivated people, the sort who relish the complexity that comes from change, thrive on the challenge.

Promoting Job Changes. Sometimes employees do not wait for the boss to suggest change—they switch themselves. Louis Gerstner, chair and CEO of IBM, is intrinsically motivated by change. He is credited with bringing IBM back from the brink of disaster; some would say that he had achieved the same outcome with RJR Nabisco four years before. In a 1996 television interview Gerstner was asked, "What's next?" In his typically straightforward way, he spoke of his attraction to new challenges—what he called "repotted careers"—and admitted he was most likely ready for another challenge. Growth, creativity, and stretching come from such change. He was not threatened by change; rather he was intrigued and intrinsically motivated by the possibility of some additional complexity that needed to be understood.

Another example of a repotted career comes from the U.S. Army. The military has always pursued the policy of transferring officers to different kinds of positions in order to prepare them for the probability that they will need a wide variety of skills and experiences to be successful. One outstanding sample of this practice is illustrated by Bernard Loeffke, Major General (retired).

Loeffke, who speaks Russian, Chinese, French, and a number of other languages, was a Ranger and a member of the original Special Forces known for being the most versatile army unit. All members of the Special Forces were required to have two military specialties and one specialty that could be employed to help civilians in war zones. Loeffke chose to become a registered midwife.

When he retired, he decided to repot himself by taking paramedical training and then becoming a physician's assistant. In addition, he is still training executives and going on special missions such as working with the people helping with the peace agreement in Ireland and in Sudan, where he recently served as a medical officer. Repotting leads to bringing a fresh pair of eyes to a problem and an energized employee.

Loeffke's repotting did not benefit his original employer (although the knowledge and experiences he gained as a midwife undoubtedly broadened his understanding of how to relate to individuals and how to value the experience of birth and life), but his Special Forces experiences enhanced his ability to thrive in the new situation in which he found himself working as a physician's assistant, and his army and medical experiences contributed to his abilities as an executive trainer and peace negotiator.

Encouraging Periods of Renewal

Repotting and role changing enable a person to get out of static relationships and worn-out patterns and approach a different position with renewed vigor and motivation. Often such moving around is not possible, so companies need to provide employees with opportunities for renewal while staying within their positions. Sabbaticals and retreats can fill this role.

Sabbaticals

Within academia and the military, sabbaticals are common and well established as a source of physical and psychological renewal. The idea is not as often used in business, but there is no reason it should not be, and in fact it is increasingly common. Hallmark exposes its employees to new thinking and new skills through what we might call internal sabbaticals, in which artists are given time to learn about and experiment with a new medium (we look at this program in depth in Chapter Six).

A human resource consulting firm has recently designed sabbaticals for the Ralston Purina Company and Nike, as Katherine Mieszkowski reported in an article in *Fast Company* (1998), referring to these periods away from normal work as "radical sabbaticals." Participants say they use the time to challenge their life assumptions and reinvent themselves. Some travel, while others work on their interpersonal skills. As they become more common, sabbaticals must change their form to provide the contrasting jolt needed to take a person out of the old rut and onto new and different pathways.

Retreats

Retreats satisfy a similar purpose. They may take place over a day or a weekend or sometimes even longer. They are usually held at a site very different from the office—a resort, a facility in the countryside, a luxurious hotel in the city.

The idea behind them is that in such a different, relaxed environment, people drop their armor and fears and feel free to strategize in creative new ways. Activities that promote this (relaxation exercises, group games, visioning, using metaphorical thinking and analogies, for example) are often part of retreats.

Once employees open up to new ideas that come from exploration, they want to explore more—this is a beneficial cycle. But there can be drawbacks, too, and these can hinder widespread receptivity to Positive Turbulence.

Mitigating Difficulties

Because of the forceful and often disruptive nature of Positive Turbulence, an organization may have barriers that keep its members from understanding and being able to work with it. Employees can become frustrated with the slow rate of change; they can decide that other pastures are greener and move on; those encouraged to have free-ranging ideas may feel isolated from the rest of the organization. But there are steps that managers can take to be aware of the pitfalls of Positive Turbulence and to avoid them.

Balancing Needs

Not everyone in a company is going to embrace Positive Turbulence. Sometimes personality and predilections get in the way of fully appreciating and accepting Positive Turbulence. The task for the savvy manager in this situation is to balance the needs of all members of the organization so that those who take off with the turbulence are not frustrated by being kept back to accommodate those who do not and that this latter group is not exasperated and even intimidated by the speed with which the others are moving.

It comes down to a question of balancing needs—of those who are most curious with those who are least curious, and of those who are most desirous of change with those who are least desirous. The point is to appreciate the opposites, because each must exist within the organization.

The Most and Least Curious. When employees are encouraged to think and see in fresh ways and are given opportunities to do so, curiosity is piqued. Those who may be curious by nature thrive in this environment and are stimulated to keep their exploration at a high fervor. At the other extreme are those who have a reduced sense of curiosity; they prefer to stay within known boundaries. They do good, dependable work, but it is generally not recognized because it does not stand out as being different. Organizations generally need both sorts of individuals, as well as those who fall in between. The key is keeping the more curious challenged and the less curious appreciated so that they do not feel neglected.

In mature industries it is often more difficult to keep motivation and curiosity at a high level; in leading-edge companies, such as those in high tech and multimedia, everything is changing at such a rapid pace that that is not the case. Managers are responsible for being attuned to their employees' needs and ensuring that in the exuberance to promote Positive Turbulence, the needs of the less receptive are not overlooked.

Those Most Desirous and Least Desirous of Change. As in the case of curiosity, an individual's desire for change can range from the fanatical to the fearful. Change leads to renewal, and renewal is the goal of Positive Turbulence, so change is something an organization wants. However, individuals within a company who thrive on change, who are driven by it, can create chaos around them, with sometimes disastrous consequences. When change for the sake of change is what is motivating an employee, difficulties are in store. At the other extreme are those who are resistant to change, often because the familiar is so comfortable and doing things differently from how they have always done them is confusing and threatening.

Again, the manager's job is to sense the pulse of change and make sure that those who for legitimate reasons desire change are not held back, and that those who are uncomfortable with it are shielded as much as possible from it or gradually prepared to accept it.

Preventing Isolation

In a company where Positive Turbulence is practiced in a limited or even minimal way, it is often up to a small group within the company to keep the waves of renewal flowing. Sometimes an individual within a department takes on this role. These are usually the highly imaginative and creative people whose free-ranging ideas pour forth, often to the astonishment (and frequently misunderstanding and dismissal) of others. In companies such as this where there may be a broad divergence between a person's or a group's innate urge toward change and the corporate culture, it is important to prevent these individuals filled with the energy of Positive Turbulence from feeling isolated or ostracized.

Positive Turbulence is an appropriate process for all companies that want to be sustainable. Leaders should be supportive of those within the organization who are constantly approaching problems from new angles, tossing out wild ideas, reading everything they can get their hands on, requesting funding for research, conferences, books and periodicals. If these people are discouraged, their resources cut off, their jobs terminated, the company loses out on the new possibilities they offer, and with that the chance for organizational renewal. Not only should these people be allowed to work in their unique style that makes use of Positive Turbulence, but they should be considered highly valuable members of the organization. In some instances they need to be buffered from the part of the organization that would be threatened by their work and does not understand the value of their style.

Retaining Employees

Any organization that exposes its employees to other companies, other fields, and other industries, as is done by encouraging them to attend conferences, join external networks, and read materials outside their area of expertise, runs the risk that their best people may be tempted to leave and join one of these other companies. When you send them off traveling, they may not want to come back, even though their term abroad is over. With all the exploration Positive Turbulence requires that they do, they may just want to repot their careers right out of your company.

These are indeed risks. You can reduce them by keeping open lines of communication with these employees so that you can help them create in their jobs what they may find so appealing about another company. You can make it easy for them to change roles within your company, if that is what they wish.

Ultimately, however, a company in which Positive Turbulence thrives is an exciting, challenging, invigorating, creative one, and the more freedom an individual has to respond to Positive Turbulence, the more content these highly creative employees will be and the more likely it is that they will stay.

Avoiding Negative Turbulence

It is all too clear that turbulence can have a very destructive effect if it is not managed well. Negative Turbulence, in which status quo becomes the safest response to new information, affects the organization's ability to respond to challenge. The climate is no longer energizing and snuffs out the fires of renewal.

When people sense that the organization is engaging in change for the sake of change or when the end result feels like overload, those are sure indicators that turbulence has become negative. In that poisoned climate, nothing good can be achieved.

Creative leaders must exert all effort toward ensuring that the turbulence they invite in stays positive. They must build a basis for acceptance of it through all the ways discussed in this chapter. They must understand turbulence in all its forms and be attuned to any deleterious impacts it may have on employees. At the same time they bring the turbulence into the organization, never fully knowing in advance just how it will interact with employees, they need to monitor and gauge and control its effect at each step of the way.

Most people get their best information and ideas not by reading the journals in their own field, not even by going to conferences targeted to their own specialization, but by happening to meet someone in a group of open-minded individuals who says something that starts a train of thought rolling toward an unknown destination. Much of our best information hits us on a tangent. All we have to do is make sure that we are ready when it happens.

Receptivity to Positive Turbulence sets up an energetic and self-perpetuating cycle, building on its own momentum. It broadens employees' knowledge and experience, and they become more accepting of new ideas and information. When they adopt this new information, changes come to the company in the form of renewal, and that generates yet more Positive Turbulence by catalyzing new thoughts and ideas among other employees.

Chapter Four

Strategies for Developing Positive Turbulence in Teams

Teams are ubiquitous in business today. As a structural unit for getting things done, teams have accomplished near-miracles in many companies. High-performing work teams have made major turnarounds in productivity. Problem-solving teams have come up with brilliant solutions for dilemmas that had stubbornly resisted the efforts of management. New product teams have developed sophisticated widgets that thrust the company into entirely new and profitable markets.

There are self-managed work teams, design teams, R&D teams, task forces, executive committees, even the very modern variation of virtual teams that never sit at the same table in the same time zone. What teams usually share in common is that members have a breadth of experiences, skills, strengths, perspectives, and views of the world that can be brought to bear on the task at hand. Collectively the team is able to draw on talents that are not available to any one individual (except for rare minds such as Albert Einstein and da Vinci, but we have not seen their likes for a while).

Teams by their very nature are breeding grounds for firecracker brainstorming. The synergy produced as bright people tackle something together almost guarantees a high level of creativity. Teams are ideal groups for developing and maximizing Positive Turbulence because they can be set up in such a way that they engender creativity. Understanding how teams function is important because the lessons they reveal about Positive Turbulence can be applied to many different situations and at all company levels.

Looking at What Constitutes a Team

Teams are partly defined by size. They are generally smaller than groups and should be only as large as they need to be to get the job done and to be effectively managed by the leader. In fact size can vary from five to seven people to hundreds, depending on the nature of the task. Thomas Jefferson suggested that two hundred was the largest practical number of people who could function effectively in some significant degree while still maintaining the sense of an integrated unit. Bob Swiggett (1992), former president of Kollmorgen Corporation, then a supplier of submarine periscopes, agrees, but with a caveat: "When the division president cannot know about the spouses and children of his/her employees, much less their names, then there is trouble. I think it is very important that this family sense, their sense of unity, be there."

The more critical issue that separates teams from groups is the amount of interdependence—the degree to which the team functions as an integrated unit. The success of well-functioning work teams is directly related to how cohesively and efficiently team members work together. Every member depends on all other members; everyone knows that they can accomplish their task only by working together.

Merely calling a group of workers "a team" does not make it so. Teams are defined by three principal characteristics:

- The team members have a shared purpose, which meets a particular need.
- Members work interactively and are interdependent.
- By working together, the members learn how to enhance the team's performance.

In addition, teams often have an agreed-on task that has measurable results, and members usually consider themselves as being part of a team.

Because of their limited size and the cohesiveness that they generally exhibit, teams are able to handle more problems—and more complex problems—than groups, which often tend to be less focused and therefore less creative. When team size increases, roles become more differentiated and specialized.

Teams also have tremendous advantage over individuals. Although there are some who believe that talented individuals, working alone, will outproduce a team made up of an equal number of people every time, I am convinced that established teams have the edge when it comes to creativity and what that creativity leads to.

There are practical reasons for this advantage. Some tasks require more than two hands, no matter how skilled those hands may be. The more complex the business problem is, the more difficult it is to resolve through a linear series of actions, and the less likely it is that good solutions will spring from one brain. Implementation is another point. Single individuals, unless they happen to own the company, are seldom in a position to ram an idea through to fruition. A team united behind its proposal is a much stronger advocate. Furthermore, the elements of quality, productivity, efficiency, and effectiveness must also be added to the equation.

Through a strong sense of cohesion, support, and intellectual synergy, teams can produce highly original work. Under the influence of Positive Turbulence, their creativity is enhanced. A reciprocal relationship is also at play here. Teams benefit and use Positive Turbulence, and they also stimulate Positive Turbulence by providing their organizations with unique ideas, smart solutions, and the best collective thinking from the brightest minds.

Helping Teams Develop Positive Turbulence

Teams are not automatically, magically effective. A number of teams, beset by atrophy, entropy, paralysis, petty jealousies, lack of resources, or fading commitment, have failed to live up to their promise. But if the precepts of Positive Turbulence are followed and adapted specifically for use in teams, Positive Turbulence can rejuvenate and invigorate them.

Maintaining a Diverse Membership

The single most important strategy for enhancing creativity in teams is deliberately building in cross-fertilization by selecting members with a broad range of skills and backgrounds. The stimulation that comes from exposure to new perspectives invariably produces new ideas—though not without the challenge of having to look at and question another's viewpoint or way of doing things. When team members come from different functional units, have complementary personality styles, regularly rotate in new members, and invite in outside speakers as experts, cross-fertilization is automatic.

Including Members from Different Functional Divisions. The most obvious way to ensure diversity is to include on the team members from several different functional units in the company—manufacturing, marketing, finance, human resources, design, and so forth. We usually think of cross-functional teams most often in connection with new product development, but there is no reason the same philosophy cannot be used happily with other sorts of teams.

Teams assembled to design new products are most critically in need of the input from many functions. It has been generally accepted that 60 percent of the cost of manufacturing anything is built in at the design stage. (When I quoted that statistic to a group of managers from General Motors recently, they laughed and said the figure was too low.) If the people with expertise in the manufacturing processes are not sitting at the table when the thing is designed, it is a good bet that cost efficiencies are lost.

General Electric recognizes this. According to an article in *Business Week* (Coy, Billups, and Hansen, 1995), GE gathers cross-functional groups, labeled "one-coffee-pot" teams, of employees from R&D, manufacturing, and marketing to identify and overcome obstacles to new product development. Acknowledging the importance of this sort of intragroup cooperation, GE's chair and CEO, Jack Welch, has included among its reward recipients those groups that perform well together, moving products and processes between each other.

The automobile industry provides another strong example of making use of teams comprising members from different functional divisions. Customers expect new models and new designs every year, but carmakers have enormous capital investment in their manufacturing facilities, and even minor design changes can necessitate major retooling. If manufacturing people are involved early in the product development cycle, they can provide ideas that simplify the mechanics without losing the appeal of the new design. Someone might chime in, "We can't make this kind of thing in our plant without a lot of trouble, and it's way too costly to outsource it. But if we could just make one little adjustment—say, if we use laminated plastic instead of this sheet metal—it would still do what you want and look just as snazzy, but we could make it a whole lot cheaper." Good solution. Done.

Rarely in these competitive times do companies have the luxury of taking all the time they want to perfect a new product idea. There is usually a brief period when the timing is optimal. How big that window of opportunity is depends on whom you ask. At the Center for Creative Leadership I teach a course in implementing innovation for cross-functional teams, and I always start by asking all the participants to write down what they mean by "short term." People from research generally write "two or three years"; marketing people write "two or three months." Clearly it is important to share these different perspectives early in the process and then try to use this shared knowledge in a positive way. Communicating these differences is more than half the battle, and if it is done early rather than late, negative fallout can be avoided.

Here is an amusing story about the negative consequences that ensued when three members of a cross-functional team from Milliken did not communicate their differences at an early stage. The team members—one from marketing, another from manufacturing, and the third from development—had gone to the company's lodge for a weekend of bear hunting.

Just before dawn their first morning in the lodge, Mr. Marketing and Mr. Manufacturing were awakened by the sounds of their colleague screaming from outside the lodge. Looking out their windows, they saw Mr. Development being chased by a bear, both running as fast as they could. When they somewhat recovered their senses, they realized that what their coworker was yelling was, "Open the door!"

So they devised a plan. They would stand just behind the door, and when they heard the footsteps of Mr. Development—by this time rounding the pond in front of the lodge—coming up the wooden stairs, they would open the door just long enough for their colleague to run in. They would then slam it before Mr. Bear could run into Milliken Lodge.

As Mr. Development was making his way around the pond, the other two managers practiced the maneuver. Then the real test came. They opened the door at just the right moment, but because Mr. Development had not been privy to their plan, he ran in and then stood in such a way that he blocked the access of his colleagues to the door. In ran Mr. Bear. Having had all he wanted of his ursine pursuer, Mr. Development grabbed the door handle, ran outside, and slammed the door behind him, calling out to his colleagues, "You skin this one. I'll find another."

This story was related by the divisional president of Milliken at one of my courses on cross-functional teams. As the laughter in the room subsided, he concluded, saying by way of explaining his participation in the course, "And that is how product development *currently* happens in our organization."

Incorporating Complementary Personality Styles. Cross-functionality is a source of Positive Turbulence in teams, but it is not always possible. Certain teams, because of their mission, must contain people from just one function or one discipline. But you can still create sparks that can then generate Positive Turbulence by including on those teams people with different but complementary (to maintain the cohesiveness of the group) personalities.

Team members may differ from one another in their personal styles, life experiences, cultural backgrounds, problem-solving styles—even in terms of Jungian personality typology. The idea is that when different types of people are present, an atmosphere of creative tension prevails, out of which will come—presumably—good ideas.

David Welty, director of new product development at Hall-mark, found this to be the case. He uses Jungian typology to put together his team and finds that when the resulting diversity of thinking is combined with ongoing training, "It seems to result in very positive turbulence."

Nissan Design International, in putting together its design team, hires "divergent pairs" to address issues from distinct orientations, which has resulted in a variety of design styles being generated. "We have found ourselves more open to candidates representing a significantly greater range of cognitive styles, professional approaches, and personal idiosyncrasies," says NDI's Jerry Hirshberg (1998).

Rotating in New Members. Another way to guarantee a fresh perspective in a team is through the device of bringing in a new person at set intervals—six months is a good period. This is especially appropriate for teams that are going to be working together for a long time. When the new person comes in, an old member may or may not leave; the team itself will have to decide if it can accommodate the ever-increasing size.

The new person has one primary function, and all the existing members must accept it without rancor. This person's job is to continually ask, "Why are we doing it this way?" The rest of the team knows that this will create some disruption, but it will force them to rethink some issues and clarify their process.

After six months have passed, the new member will be fully integrated into the team, and no longer thinks to ask the question. That is about the time another new person will come in, to continue the process of challenging and nudging by asking, "Why?"

Bringing in Outside Experts

There is value in bringing in people who are experts in some field outside the normal business of the company. The intellectual stimulation of being exposed to new and different ideas produces mental fireworks that can sometimes lead to amazing innovations in the company. Or not. Sometimes it leads only to the fun of thinking about ideas and processes in a brand-new way. And all strong leaders know just how valuable that kind of fun can be to the creative organization.

The same energizing process can be used very successfully with teams. In fact, it is somewhat easier to manage with teams, for the "visiting experts" may be found very close at hand, in other areas of the company. Remember that all along we have been talking about opening up the sight lines to the periphery, where the early hints of new trends are building. In a team the periphery is the edge of the team itself. It may well be that projects and processes going on elsewhere in the company can trigger new ideas for solving the team's task. The lesson for teams is to search out other people doing interesting things and hang out with them. This is one benefit of the internal idea exchange I have called corporationwide trade shows, described in Chapter Five.

But even if those formal systems are not in place, the team members on their own are often empowered to call on the talents and the brash ideas of outsiders. If nothing else, they can take a cue from the legendary Bell Laboratories, cited in *Fortune* magazine (Farnham, 1994), which expects its research scientists to eat lunch in the dining room—not alone at their desks—and to engage in energized conversations with folks from other sections of the company.

Promoting Intensity

The intensity of turbulence—its speed, volume, and force—properly managed, is an essential component of Positive Turbulence. In teams, where the players are fewer and expectations higher, that intensity holds an even more important role. Without it, projects can fizzle and motivation dwindle. But creating deadlines—self-imposed or dictated by necessity—and focusing solutions charges up the group's energy and concentrates it fully on the project at hand.

Creating Deadlines. Every one of us has experienced the galvanizing force of deadlines: when the thing has to be done and time is running out, somehow we manage to do it. That little bit of human nature can be turned to advantage in teams as a source of turbulence.

Some teams begin with an established time frame and a definite end point that is built into their organizing charter. The pressure of the deadline forces them to stay focused on solutions. Whether the time pressure results in better or weaker solutions has to do with all the other variables in the team; here our concern is a device for keeping everyone on the same track.

Recognizing the benefits of deadlines, some team leaders have been known to create artificial deadlines for their tasks, which is what Thomas Edison apparently did (Millard, 1993). It was said that whenever he found himself profoundly blocked, he announced to the press that he would produce "a minor invention every ten days and a big thing every six months." The time pressures gave him the tension needed to unstick his thinking so that a breakthrough of new ideas would be forthcoming. In today's fast-moving world, we hardly need artificial deadlines; the real ones are usually motivation enough.

Focusing the Solution. In searching for a solution, teams, and especially very creative ones, have a tendency to let loose with ideas, spraying them all over the place. Results can range from useful and appropriate solutions, to lots of useless ideas, to useful ideas for other projects but not the one in need of a solution. With a deadline looming, that scattershot approach may not work.

At the Center for Creative Leadership I developed a model for idea generation to help teams be more efficient and more effective at thinking creatively. It teaches group idea generation skills, but in a way that is quite different from other idea generation techniques. We call this model Targeted Innovation (TI). It suggests the simple yet radical idea that creativity is predictable.

What is unique about TI is its highly focused nature. Rather than turning the team loose, you determine ahead of time what kind of solution is required for the problem at hand. What you get fits what you need, instead of simply a good idea that may or may not have anything to do with the problem of the moment. You are then concentrating a large amount of energy and attention on a specific target—in a sense, managing the intensity.

Thus, if a team determines that what it needs is a low-cost modification of an earlier process, the TI model has techniques that will generate a high percentage of ideas that fall into that category. In comparison, if the team knows it needs a long-term idea—something that is quite different and does not fit the standards already in place—the model also has techniques that, in a very predictable way, produce a high percentage of ideas that fall into the category of doing things differently. The model takes the team where it needs to be. That is why we say it is very efficient: it enables the team to use the time it has available for idea generation efficiently.

At the same time that it increases efficiency, this tool builds in Positive Turbulence. Incorporated into the model are multiple steps that guarantee cross-communication between participants. This inevitably forces team members to think differently about the problem, which leads to their generating more creative ideas. TI is especially useful in teams because it focuses the potential creativity of a group of people who not only have to generate the ideas but implement them as well. (For a more detailed description of Targeted Innovation and how to use it, turn to Appendix B.)

Directing Intensity. We have all experienced situations that have required extraordinary efforts; in the aftermath we are often astounded at how we managed to rise to the occasion. Often it is the need of the moment—usually a crisis—that prompts such unusual efforts. What often makes the difference between success and failure in such a situation is that there are people in control who are able to direct the intensity everyone is experiencing into proper channels for an expeditious and efficacious resolution of the crisis. We see a very clear example of this in Chapter Six, when we look at how Norfolk Southern responded to the ravages of Hurricane Camille, which in 1969 brought the railroad's main line between Atlanta and Washington, D.C., to a standstill.

Encouraging Frequent Interactions

When you increase the opportunities for interaction between and among individuals on a team, you increase the likelihood that sparks will fly and new ideas burst forth. Sometimes these interactions should be arranged, as in the case of daily staff meetings; more often they should be spontaneous, as takes place in informal meeting spaces.

Holding Daily Staff Meetings. Most of us dread meetings, which we see as a not terribly productive use of time. Nevertheless, regular meetings are imperative for teams, where cohesiveness and collaboration are basic to the group's success. Meetings bring the group together, let everyone know what everyone else is doing, and foster strategizing together. Daily meetings reinforce the importance of the group and provide a daily venue for idea generation and problem solving. By keeping the meetings short and focused (remember how to direct intensity) and by reinforcing direction and motivation, you generate Positive Turbulence.

At Mead Central Research, part of Mead Paper Company, a leading manufacturer and distributor of school supplies and paper-based products for the home and office, the advanced product development group held daily staff meetings in the hallways. The idea behind them, according to Dick Wright (1992), the group's manager, was to keep the information churning (what's new today) and to keep attention focused and interest high. Team members made quick announcements, asked targeted questions, and suggested different directions for potential solutions. If more time was needed, smaller groups with the appropriate people continued the discussion.

Wright pioneered this process because he believed that generally a collaborative team can allow more diversity and antonymy than one that clings together for mutually distrustful motives. From this philosophy came his innovative management style of spending the majority of his time with his subordinates on their turf—listening to them and being involved yet not meddling. His "walking-around" style then led to the hallway meetings.

These meetings benefited both the team and the company. Because the meetings became part of the team culture, they helped instill a sense of positive group identity. Furthermore, they aided communication among members. Because the leader communicated so openly with the group, other members began to do the same; technicians began to open up too. And because the teams' meetings were held out in the open, with anyone free to listen in, the groups' issues and business at hand were accessible to anyone who wanted to be informed.

Setting Aside Informal Meeting Spaces.   Some enlightened companies set aside alcoves or small areas where informal—and usually inspirational—chats can take place. Think of an occasion when you bumped into someone in the corridor, had a brief discussion, and in that casual environment some amazing discussions took place. You felt free to offer off-the-wall (quite literally) suggestions because you were unconstrained by the formality of a meeting, with its agenda and expectations.

Some forward-thinking organizations change internal traffic patterns and architects' designs to include such informal spaces that Nancy Dixon (1997) refers to as hallways of learning. Our new building at the Center for Creative Leadership includes "serendipity space"—alcoves off to the side of heavily trafficked hallways—where people who have met in the hall can sit down and follow through on the hallway connection.

Using Technology

One of the computer companies that provides consumers with high-tech products concluded a recent series of television commercials with this high-spirited tag line: "Is this a great time, or what?"

Is it ever! In an amazingly short time, we have come to accept, even take for granted, the wonders of sophisticated technology (e-mail, voice mail, videoconferencing) for all sorts of daily communication, both business and personal. The Internet provides research capability, entertainment, and a sense of connectedness that is vastly different from what our parents knew, not only in its format and speed of delivery, but in its essential spirit.

The speed that technology affords and the almost limitless wealth of information people have access to through using it make technology a great tool for both paying attention to the periphery and increasing the intensity of Positive Turbulence. In the case of teams, advances in communications technology make it possible for people working in different locations to become a team in every respect other than physical proximity. Geographically dispersed through several countries and many time zones, they are nonetheless a team—a virtual team—because of the shared work they do. With new software, they are able to come to group decisions electronically.

Creating Virtual Teams. Virtual teams are in evidence in almost every industry and every aspect of business operation; global markets and offshore manufacturing facilities make it a necessity. Of particular interest for this chapter are research teams and other teams focused on innovations.

Because of the complex maze of legal, tax, and copyright concerns, together with domestic and foreign regulatory issues, it is becoming common for organizations to locate some of their research laboratories outside the United States. A pharmaceutical company, for instance, may have its corporate headquarters in the United States and sales centers around the globe, but its main research facility is in Europe and additional research facilities are located in Latin America. People from these locations may work on a cross-functional geographically dispersed development team yet have the same interdependency as other teams and the same need for insightful communication. Because half of the team sleeps in Europe, a quarter in Latin America, and a quarter in Asia, they depend on technology—e-mail, network capabilities, and videoconferencing, for example—to make it possible.

Using Group Decision-Making Software. Several types of group decision-making software offer an electronic way for allowing teams to grow and still feel interconnected. The examples I have seen are conferences of any number of people, spread around the world, communicating in real time (or asynchronously) via networked laptop computers. At any given moment, they can see three or four ideas on the screen in front of them, followed instantly by comments and reactions from several other participants.

The great advantage of this technique is the anonymity. Participants see only the ideas popping in and out; they do not know who the authors are. It could be the boss or someone they consider a screwball. They can react only to the validity of the idea itself, free of political considerations. Although these programs were originally conceived as a tool for making decisions, they also have great potential for a group process of generating new ideas.

Maintaining Team Effectiveness

Consider for a moment a very familiar object—your car. It may surprise you to learn that the automobile is not a highly efficient device for transporting people and goods. Even in a well-designed and carefully maintained automobile, only about 15 percent of the total energy that is created by burning the gasoline is available for actually moving the car forward. The rest is lost to heat, friction, air resistance, and other aspects of the laws of physics that the design of the engine must take into account. However, even less-than-efficient combustion engines have their place. If you need to pick up some plywood or transport a soccer team, a bicycle will not suffice.

Teams are somewhat the same. It is unrealistic to expect a team, especially at start-up, to deliver its total capacity—the combined abilities of the full assemblage of people. In fact, a team is always capable of doing more than it is actually doing, because there is no way to bring all of its capabilities to focus. A team that is running at 50 percent efficiency, measured against what it could do if called on, is doing very well indeed.

Teams can do amazing things, especially if we can find ways to diminish some of the problems that inevitably arise by allowing Positive Turbulence to keep them moving forward. Some solutions are keeping members from thinking alike, balancing focus with awareness of both the periphery and the rest of the company, keeping arrogance at bay, and preventing a sense of isolation among members.

Avoiding Uniformity.   One of the catch-22s of organizational reality that has particular relevance to teams is that with efficiency comes loss of spontaneity and creativity. With teams, this problem is often referred to as "uniformity pressure"—the tendency of individual team members to act and think alike. It derives usually from a pressure (felt or actual) to conduct themselves efficiently (meaning efficiency of action), and to be perceived and to perceive themselves as a high-performing team producing high-quality work.

The commonly understood way to achieve this efficiency is through focus, which in a team setting means people moving in sync with each other in terms of their understanding, the way they frame the problem, and the process they are using. Unfortunately for their creativity, the more in sync they are, the less room there is for unexpected behavior and new thoughts. Paradoxically, it is the most efficient teams that are most vulnerable to developing these particular blinders.

In *The Wisdom of Teams* (1993), Jon Katzenbach suggests that if the team is regularly challenged with fresh facts and information, it can avoid uniformity of thinking. If you think of the fresh facts and information as coming from the periphery, then by following some of the practices of Positive Turbulence that we discussed earlier, such as reading outside one's discipline or traveling to different places, team members can reinvigorate their individual thinking and avoid keeping the team following just one line of thought.

Avoiding Tunnel Vision. When a team is solely focused on its task, completely ignoring the outside world is just a short step away, which for members is everything beyond the team's boundary. But as we know, the outside world is the source of new ideas. Intense focus on the team's work—the very thing that makes the team successful—can eventually turn into a liability if team members unconsciously shut themselves off from new ideas.

Being aware of this tendency is the first step in avoiding tunnel vision. Continually bringing in fresh ideas from the outside (through articles, speakers, and managers from other areas) can underscore the notion that good ideas come from all over, whether the periphery or the interstices of the organization. Rotating in new team members who bring their own perspectives can also help prevent tunnel vision.

Preventing Isolation. The best teams have a high degree of cohesion, a high energy level, and a culture of support. That is teamwork, by definition: a higher degree of involvement in the work than each person would have working alone, and a strong sense of connectedness to each other and to the team itself, as its own entity.

However, we are a competitive culture, and the positive side of teams can easily disintegrate into a negative and unproductive degree of competition with other teams, other divisions of the company, senior management, or anyone else perceived as interfering with the glory of the team. "We're number one," which just might be a national mantra, often slides into an us-versus-them mentality.

The very behaviors that make teams successful, that lead to good performance and high morale, can also lead to arrogance, or at least the perception of it. Then it is but a short step to jealousy and even sabotage from other individuals and other teams. Not a pretty picture.

Maintaining a balance between a healthy sense of pride in a team's accomplishments and a sense of arrogance can be difficult. Because teams are by their very nature special, members can be so focused on their own importance and own sense of accomplishment that they become arrogant. The repercussions of this behavior can extend beyond the team's process and eventually affect people's view of the team.

Team leaders (or senior managers, in the case of self-managed teams) must be ever on guard against insularity and the competitiveness that it breeds. By highlighting the accomplishments of other groups and introducing speakers who are equally creative, energetic, and accomplished, team members can perhaps learn a bit of humility. This then is what keeps them from being ostracized and ultimately isolated, and, worst case, their work even ignored.

Setting Up a Positive Turbulence-Driven Team in a Turbulence-Averse Company

Not all companies readily adapt Positive Turbulence to their company culture. Some organizations that seek creativity are not always willing to accept dramatic change. In others, even supposed centers of creativity like corporate R&D functions are often hampered by a corporate structure that impedes feedback on and approval of creative ideas coming out of the group.

Nevertheless, groups within such organizations have been able to establish themselves in ways that capitalize on the strategies of Positive Turbulence. The results—innovations that are embraced by the company—are what gain acceptance of these teams and ensure their longevity, while not necessarily prompting the company to embrace the tenets of Positive Turbulence. The Office of Innovation at Eastman Kodak Company and Microsoft Research, commonly known as "Bill Labs," are examples of two such teams.

They are essentially parallel organizations that exist outside the main hierarchical structures of their parent companies.

Kodak's Office of Innovation

In its early days, beginning in 1979, the Office of Innovation occupied just one room and had a remarkable leader, Bob Rosenfeld (1983), who was initially a research scientist in the laboratory. He believed that creativity would ensue if people were nurtured, especially in the early stages of idea development, and that support for this creativity should come from the manager and the infrastructure.

On the door to the room that housed the Office of Innovation was this sign:

Office of Innovation Philosophy.

Ideas are fragile (and so are people).

Ideas are organic and need to be nurtured (and so do people).

Only potentially valuable ideas will be brought to management for a decision.

Through consultation with experts the spark of truth will emerge.

The office's purpose was to select innovative ideas at the early stages, evaluate them for potential merit, and then find sponsorship or a champion for them from within the mainstream organization. In accord with the sign on the door, the group's philosophy was based on three premises:

- Ideas that lie outside the scientists' immediate job assignments are given a fair hearing.
- The office taps into the diversity of talent in the company (or even outside) to build ideas into viable proposals that can be sponsored internally or sold or licensed externally.

- The office creates a climate in which creativity and innovation flourish, unconstrained by traditional top-down management practices.

The new venture team eventually outgrew its small space. The team moved to a storefront office in downtown Rochester. This alternative structure then existed in parallel to a much larger ongoing research and development effort. It is probably only in this parallel form that the following characteristics of the group could be tolerated:

- No restrictions were placed on the type or focus of an idea.
- Participant anonymity was preserved.
- The idea originator carried the idea through to a decision.
- A facilitative, nonjudgmental process was followed.
- No external time pressure was placed on projects.
- Access to corporate expertise was available.
- Resources for idea enhancement and development were provided.
- The office facilitated the active seeking of a company sponsor.

By tapping into diversity both within and outside the organization through inviting multiple perspectives and alternative frameworks, the group provided a mechanism for enhancing receptivity to Positive Turbulence. This then increased the likelihood that an idea would find a place to be of use. By not demanding closure or resolution of an idea immediately, allowing a permissive and laissez-faire attitude with regard to the pushing of limits, tolerating half-baked ideas, and encouraging the element of play with regard to these ideas, this parallel organization showed itself to be the model of a turbulence-driven group. Its acceptance was based on the fact that ideas once considered too radical to be entertained by the mainstream were made palatable by having been through a process that transformed them into workable ideas embraced by the larger organization.

Among its accomplishments, the team developed a film recorder that produces images primarily onto large-format sheets of film, thereby revolutionizing the way digital film is exposed. Early on in the process, the group brought people from marketing into the discussion, who suggested a new direction for the product—digital retouching for the high-end graphics field that would enable art directors to have an image in hand, not just on the computer screen. The product's initiator also spent time with potential customers, finding out about their needs and how his product could fulfill them.

Both the product development team and the product were successful for a number of reasons. The team sought outside input—from other divisions, customers, people from another venture, individuals with different orientations. The team was receptive to their recommendations and willing to revise its original business plan based on that outside information. Because team members had "people skills," they were able to interact effectively with the outside people.

The Office of Innovation at Kodak created a climate in which creativity and innovation flourished, and it cohabited quite successfully with the rest of the organization, which did not embrace Positive Turbulence. Microsoft Research is a somewhat similar group.

"Bill Labs" at Microsoft

Anyone who pays even cursory attention to the history and current state of innovation in American industry knows about the research group at AT&T, popularly known as Bell Labs. The work that is done there, and the atmosphere in which it is conceived, is the stuff of legends. So when Microsoft Corporation, the mega-giant computer company headed by Bill Gates, set out to establish a world-class research unit, it was only a matter of time before media wags began to call Microsoft Research "Bill Labs."

Chief technology officer Nathan Myhrvold has led Microsoft Research from its beginning in 1991 (eons ago, in computer time). His plan was simple: bring together people from many disciplines, not just the predictable technologies, who are already engaged in some research that Microsoft might someday benefit from, give them the resources they need, set up circumstances in which they can interact with each other, and stand back out of the way. He described it this way: "It's a little like conducting a dinner party. [You don't] interrupt the conversations and tell people what they should be saying and thinking. If you pick the right people to convene, more and better things happen than you could have planned" (Stross, 1997).

Microsoft does not do anything halfway. Myhrvold has the corporate blessing—in the form of a healthy budget and unflinching support at the highest level—to do whatever it takes to build the group into a superlative research organization. There is only one condition, and it was Myhrvold himself who insisted on it: there must be an obvious benefit to the company. What they do is pure research, basic research, and some of it may not pay off for many years, but none of it is ivory-tower material.

Today the research team comprises approximately 350 of the brightest minds in many fields of science, and it plans to add 250 more by the year 2000 (Johnston, 1998). Some team members were brazenly hired away from competitors and others lured from universities around the world. They work at the main research center in Redmond, Washington (corporate headquarters), or the new laboratory in Cambridge, England, or in several small satellite offices in other cities.

Although Microsoft Research is considerably larger than most other research efforts, it demonstrates how Positive Turbulence can be developed and maximized in even large research and development organizations.

A colleague, who is also a good friend, noted on a list the characteristics he feels suggest an ideal team:

- There is a great deal of cross-fertilization among members.
- When they are communicating well, members reflect a common denominator.
- All members of the team are free to choose responsibly without needing a leader.
- Each person on the team knows how to adapt to and work with constant change.
- At times the team member must be buffered from the rest of the team.
- Members exhibit a discipline of improvisation; when they are performing at a high level, they improvise simultaneously.

Does this sound like a description of our ideal of a high-performing, self-managed, cross-functional, turbulence-driven team? It is. It was written by musician and jazz historian Bobby Bradford (Gryskiewicz, 1989), whom we met in the previous chapter and who has been observing creative people in action for more than forty years. The team he describes, however, is the ultimate jazz combo.

Chapter Five

Strategies for Managing Positive Turbulence

For Positive Turbulence to succeed at any level, it requires, at the very least, the blessings of management. For it to flourish, it must have the active support of the organization under the direction of creative leaders.

Positive Turbulence is not only a powerful process but a very challenging and confrontational one, in that it often draws from extremes—whether outsiders or change or intensity or creative performers. Because it is outside the familiar, it takes a leadership not just versed in the precepts of Positive Turbulence but completely in sync with its goals and dynamics. These leaders must be advocates, promoters, teachers, and developers of Positive Turbulence. They must be the prime gatekeepers, ushering turbulence into the organization. They must be able to make sure it is well received and productively used when it arrives, and they must be able to ensure that the winds of turbulence do not turn destructive.

A company's leadership can skillfully direct Positive Turbulence by using the periphery most propitiously, developing the appropriate corporate culture, and keeping the turbulence flowing and positive.

Making Effective Use of the Periphery

The periphery is a prime source of turbulence. Whether one brings it in or not, that pool of potentially catalyzing information and ideas flows past an organization. It is up to the astuteness of a group's leaders as to how well or poorly the turbulence will be used.

In Chapter Three we looked at how to broaden one's peripheral vision by reading outside the particular field in which one works, attending conferences on far-ranging topics, and traveling. Here we look at ways to use the periphery on a companywide basis by hiring new people who bring with them fresh perspectives, inviting in outside experts who can identify significant trends, and creating cross-fertilization.

Recruiting New Talent

"I've been here so long that I can no longer see the creativity within my own organization" is a confession that only a few leaders are honest enough to utter aloud. We often fail to see the potential in our own backyards. Yet that blindness can stymie a company's ability to maintain the competitive edge. Our vision is blurred, to a degree, by familiarity and routine. One cure is to recruit someone from the outside who may be able to see in an instant how a process could be improved though no one ever really thought it needed to be, or that a time-worn structure is no longer effective, or that an employee, as we will see in the case of Weird Al, whose ideas may have been ignored really is on to something. Keeping an influx of new talent is an essential step on the road to renewal, as we see so clearly in the following account.

It was the early 1980s. A forward-looking company in a traditional industry began to think hard and long about a series of products that would take the company into the twenty-first century. Within its industry the company had a reputation for being an innovator. Could it continue to come up with products that would perpetuate that reputation?

The challenge was given to the senior director of central research, who had been with the company a long time and knew its products and its research staff well. After much consideration, he concluded that a high level of creativity existed within the laboratory, but he was too close to the existing technology to lead the search for new products. He decided to look outside the company for someone else to direct the advanced-technology group. The person he chose was not only outside the company but also slightly outside the industry.

For the first six weeks, the new manager, a scientist, was given only one charge: "Walk around this organization and get to know the people and their ideas." He quickly learned that there were strong people in the research laboratory with wide-awake minds and promising ideas, yet he saw no evidence of the Big Idea.

At the end of each week, the new manager sat down with the director and reported on his observations. By the third week, he asked his new boss a question: "Who is this guy everyone calls Weird Al? The staff suggested that I ask you about him."

The director looked uncomfortable. "Al is no longer in Central Research. I sent him over to the mill to fight production fires."

"Why?"

"Oh, well, you know, it's just . . . Al likes to have ideas, too many of them, in fact. But he never does anything with them. I figured we needed a change, and Al agreed."

The new manager was astonished. How could people charged with responsibility for creativity make such an anticreativity decision? There must be a story behind this, he thought.

Indeed there was. Weird Al and the research director, the manager learned, had started their careers with the company in the same year. Both were noted for their creativity, but the man who was now director had exhibited management skills and had moved up the management ladder, while Al chose to stay in research.

For a long time, Al and his old friend had their first cup of coffee of the day together. Feet up on the director's desk, Al chatted about his latest intriguing idea. More often than not, those morning minutes turned into hours. Eventually, realizing that Al was unlikely to act on any of his ideas, the director reassigned him to the mill, where his job was to troubleshoot production problems. He felt it was a better use of Al's time—not to mention his own.

Curious, the newcomer asked to meet with Al. So the next day, just outside the noise of the production process, the two men talked.

"Al, your friends back in Research Central tell me that you always have new ideas. Is this true?"

"Sure. As a matter of fact, I just happen to have one with me."

Al pulled a small object out of his shirt pocket and demonstrated in a very crude manner the interesting things that happened when it was used in a particular way. The manager-scientist, trying to control his excitement, asked Al to repeat what he had just done. Al did. Describing it later, the manager said simply, "I saw magic."

Other people inside the organization had seen this same demonstration but had paid little attention. It took someone with an outside perspective to recognize the possibilities.

Al, as you might imagine, was quickly moved back to Research Central, and his idea became the unique product the organization was looking for to secure its place in the next century. I cannot be more specific without violating the organization's request for confidentiality. Suffice it to say that you have seen and profited from the product that evolved from Al's idea—and would not have evolved at all were it not for the R&D director's having hired someone from the periphery and given him the freedom to act as he saw fit.

By coming in with a fresh perspective that may question how things are done, see alternative ways of doing things, and uncover overlooked resources, the newly hired, recruited from outside the organization, reverse stale patterns and reinvigorate the environment.

Bringing in Outside Experts

It is a fact of human nature that we often accord more weight to the words of outsiders than we do to our immediate colleagues. (Were this not so, the consultant industry would not exist.) In the context of Positive Turbulence, this bit of human psychology works to our advantage. For bringing us news of distant trends, it is only logical that we depend on someone from that distant environment, someone with hands-on expertise.

We have already seen that in the case of teams, a hedge against uniformity was to bring in ideas from outside experts. By bringing in outside experts to talk on something as far afield from your normal purview as Tiffany's vase was from Kettering's automobiles, you open up your employees' minds to any number of possibilities.

Bell Labs, one of the most creative sources for novel and useful ideas in the communications arena, is a prime example. Since its inception, it has averaged more than two new patents a day. In addition to hiring experts in its field and providing them with resources such as time, materials, and other talented people, Bell Labs brings to these scientists the additional good thinking found in tangentially related fields of knowledge.

Bell Labs holds a forum for this type of stimulation each month. Outsiders are invited to address the group with the sole purpose of providing some provocative thinking and even outrageous ideas to the Bell Labs scientists (Asinof, 1982). Although attendance is voluntary, this interchange has become one of the more popular Friday afternoon events at the Murray Hill, New Jersey, site. Many scientists bring their teenaged children along so the youngsters too can benefit from the topics and high-caliber presentations.

Two criteria guarantee the quality of the presentations. The first is that the person presenting be a recognized world expert in his or her field. The second, a bit more difficult, mandates that the expertise of the invited presenter not currently exist inside the laboratory itself. These two standards help ensure that a creative spark is generated. The novel ideas from the outside speakers are floated before the intrinsically motivated, bright Bell Labs employees who scan the information for linkages to their own work that can result in some imaginative and useful innovations.

On one occasion Roger Payne, a world-renowned scientist, was brought in to talk about a discovery he had made regarding the behavior of whales. He related to the group that he had noticed something no one else had—that whales exhibit a most unusual change in their language patterns from year to year, from one season to the next. The only other species he was aware of changing those patterns is humans. "But we call them 'hit tunes,'" he said (Phillips Petroleum, 1984).

This change in sound patterns, which he discovered while "fooling around," listening with his friends to tapes of humpback whales communicating with each other, led Payne to conclude that humpback whales sing. What Roger Payne brought to this discovery that perhaps others who had listened to humpbacked whales did not was his early training as an ornithologist. Birds keep the same language pattern from year to year. If you heard a mockingbird when you were two years old, and not again until you were twenty-two, the language pattern of the bird would be the same in a very predictable manner. In fact, the sound of the bird and its particular pattern is a recognition characteristic.

Halfway through Payne's animated talk, a Bell Labs scientist jumped up from his seat and returned to his laboratory. Inspired by the information about humpback whales' singing, he developed a way to improve communications during sensitive operations between and to submarines under water. Payne's passionate explanation of his discovery provided the right chemistry for breakthrough thinking. Spurred by discussion of a subject wholly outside his usual realm of focus, the scientist was able to grasp a solution he might never otherwise have uncovered.

What is also significant about this incident is that Bell Labs had the good sense to provide regular opportunities for information from the periphery—no matter how far afield—to be brought before employees with no expectation of what might result. And it took this philosophy even further. More recently, Bell Labs organized another internal lecture series. Entitled "Not Your Usual Research Seminar," it featured outside speakers and futurists with new views about the economy, consumers, and technology. This series was the brainchild of David Isenberg, the head of a unique unit known as the Opportunity Discovery Department, or ODD (Petzinger, 1998). Isenberg also published an internal newsletter, *No Surprises*, to alert senior management of potential commercial and technological trends on the periphery of Bell Labs.

ODD's purpose was to tell those at Bell Labs who would listen that the universe was beginning to suggest the direction of change and to ask them if it would not be good to know something about that direction now, perhaps before the competition did. Isenberg was combining the prework of scenario planning (described later in this chapter) with a mechanism for the internal stimulation for change—an internal mechanism for hearing the outside, which, because people listen with different sets of ears to their colleagues than they do to outsiders, can be heard only through an outsider's perspective.

Bell Labs's belief that bright, motivated scientists can turn relevant novel impulses into applied thinking capable of breaking any cognitive logjams they may be faced with reveals a true understanding and deft implementing of Positive Turbulence. Importing outside experts takes place not only at high-tech centers of excellence. In the next chapter we see how Hallmark makes use of outside experts it brings in on a regular basis.

Seizing Opportunities for Cross-Fertilization

Cross-fertilization comes about when different people work together on a daily basis. No organization needs to go halfway around the world to find that kind of stimulation. By hiring a diverse workforce and taking advantage of the different kinds of people who come together through company mergers and alliances, you can inject creative exchanges into your organization.

Hiring a Diverse Workforce. Diversity of perspective in the workplace provides a natural setting for proactive Positive Turbulence. The best way to achieve that diversity is to hire it by deliberately staffing the organization with people who bring with them different perspectives, life experiences, worldviews, cultural backgrounds, and ways of thinking.

This recommendation may seem simple and obvious, but it is not always easy to implement. There is an innate tendency to want to surround ourselves with people who are like us. But if we do so, and fail to push beyond that very comfortable arena, we miss out on some important information. Remember Skandia's planning team (described in Chapter Two) that deliberately includes three generations of individuals to provide the broadest range of views.

Today we see that same meeting of different generations all across America. Generation Xers (born between 1965 and 1981) are coming into workplaces where baby boomers (born between 1946 and 1964) as well as those born between 1925 and 1945 (called the Silent Generation) have already been working. The Xers in general are relatively comfortable with technology, have less need for status, are comfortable working in open offices, and seek a balance between their work and private life. The boomers, on the other hand, consider their jobs their lives, are less techno- logically proficient, and are more political and less diverse. Mem- bers of the Silent Generation are usually loyal to the company, respect authority, and prefer the status quo (Flynn, 1996).

According to USA Today ("Aging Boom Is at Hand," 1994), someone will be turning fifty years old every eight seconds for the next sixteen years, which will come to about 79 million middle- aged adults (Bivins, 1998), most of whom will still be working; in 1997 there were already more than 40 million Xers employed as well (Losyk, 1997). The resultant turbulence will have an interest- ing impact on the climate for creativity in the work setting. The face-off has already begun, with the Xers' resistance to hierarchy, for example, and lack of loyalty to the company coming up against the Silent Generation's steadfastness to the system and the com- pany, and their pragmatism and search for instant gratification challenging the boomers' idealism and belief that paying one's dues by putting in time will be rewarded later. We can only hope that the differences these groups manifest will result in Positive Turbu- lence for these employees and their employers.

For Positive Turbulence to be fully operative, companies need to bring together a truly diverse workforce that includes not just representatives from the different generations, but people from all over the globe, different disciplines, varied applied experiences, and different cultural and racial backgrounds. The globalization of business is certainly helping this to happen, as is the influx of foreign employees through the increasing numbers of work visas being granted to noncitizens in certain fields. Human resource departments need to understand the connection between a diverse workforce and Positive Turbulence and between Positive Turbulence and a company's ongoing success so they can gear their hiring accordingly.

Merging Companies. Nearly every week the business pages of newspapers and magazines have articles on the latest merger. Whether undertaken for strategic advantage or financial benefits, mergers offer numerous opportunities for cross-fertilization. It may come through an actual merger (WorldCom and MCI Communications, NationsBank Corporation and BankAmerica Corporation, Compaq Computer Corporation and Digital Equipment Corporation, for example) or a joint venture (Time Warner, Advance Publications Incorporated, and MediaOne Group to create Road Runner, which is meant to be the largest high-speed on-line service in the United States). The reason for the merger does not matter; a change has been initiated through which these organizations—with different perspectives, strengths, and histories—now have influence on each other. Now we have in place the possibility for turbulence.

Whether the turbulence takes a negative or positive turn has much to do with the circumstances—how the changes were implemented. (Remember the concepts of volume and difference we discussed in Chapter Two and the need for controlling the resulting intensity.) Similar cultures and climates can be merged with much less upheaval. When the two organizations share a common language and common problems, their ability to learn from each other is much easier, as I saw a few years ago when I had the opportunity to work with Scandinavian Airlines System (SAS), which is jointly owned by three countries—Denmark, Norway, and Sweden. It was during a period of joint venture with Austrian Airlines, Swissair, and Continental Airlines that I witnessed a remarkable bit of collaborative creativity. (Structurally, joint ventures are not the same as mergers, but in terms of their potential to fuel creativity, we can consider them together.)

In an effort to improve its baggage-handling capabilities, baggage handlers from SAS borrowed video cameras from the corporate training department, called on their counterparts at the other three airlines, and, playing the roles of individual pieces of luggage, filmed themselves along each step of the luggage route. Handlers lay down on the baggage belt, with the camera rolling, and filmed the entire journey, from check-in to the baggage room, and finally by cart to the correct plane. Back home in Oslo, all the handlers viewed the tape to see if they could find ways to improve their own system.

The flip side of this idea is that if the two organizations are much the same to begin with, the potential for Positive Turbulence is diminished. As Bobby Bradford, the jazz musician and jazz historian, said about the creativity that resulted in new forms of jazz groups, "You can have well behaved bands with well behaved musicians, but you may not get the creativity needed to stand your group apart from others" (Gryskiewicz, 1989).

Organizational leaders are well advised to consider the wisdom in Bradford's remark as they work to merge two entities into one. The worst case, where the two organizations are extremely similar, would be total overlap and redundancy without a single spark of creativity (remember the earlier discussion of uniformity). The best case, with an optimal degree of difference, would be synergy, successful collaboration, and new approaches to long-standing problems.

Consider the case of Boeing's acquisition of McDonnell Douglas Corporation, both giants in the aircraft industry. In commenting on the proposed $13.3 billion acquisition, the new chair of Boeing, Philip M. Condit, said, "Together, we will have a wonderful balance." An article on the proposed merger in the *New York Times* reported that "when Mr. Condit runs meetings, he searches for opinions from areas of expertise different from his own" (Bryant, 1997). Sounding like a true practitioner of Positive Turbulence, Condit told the reporter, "There's a lot of information out there.

That means you've got to make an environment where people are willing to tell you. So don't shoot the messenger."

I would assert that Condit knows about Positive Turbulence and the source in which to find it. He is on record as having offered a Golden Ears Award to employees whose listening skills led to innovations. He led the development of the famous production team that produced the Boeing 777. This team set the industry standard for technology and for management by developing a process for working with a large project team.

Perhaps learning from past history will give this newly merged organization an advantage, but we must not be so naive as to expect that the companies will work together as one from the beginning. The same *New York Times* article also reported major differences within the new megacompany that posed the potential for some Negative Turbulence. McDonnell Douglas is itself a hybrid company comprising Douglas Aircraft, which builds commercial aircraft in California, and McDonnell Aircraft, which builds military aircraft in St. Louis; and although the merger took place thirty years ago, this still echoes an internal schism. How much of this will carry over to this new combined entity? Will these historical givens result in turbulence that is negative or positive?

Forging Alliances. One of the best strategies for making cross-connections between creative people from different realms is the formation of business alliances. This new form of partnering between organizations, with its roots in global economic forces, enables smaller companies to compete with the giants, make money, and stay vital. Small companies that form alliances are able to leverage expertise and share costs, such as marketing and distribution.

I experienced this firsthand when I worked with SAS. The airline was seeking a partnering relationship with airlines of similar scale and with other travel-related industries such as hotels and limousine services so it could compete with the major European carriers by offering a more complete travel experience.

Jan Carlson, the steward for this initiative, was known for bringing down the pyramids of management in favor of a more flattened and participatory work environment. At SAS his leadership brought new life to the company and to the industry. By suggesting that partnering between carriers was indeed possible and perhaps the only way to compete with the megarivals, especially with the dropping of protectionism and the coming of the more open competition in 1992 in Europe, he departed from the conventional wisdom of his industry. Today partnering and code sharing are quite common in the airline industry.

As the SAS experience demonstrates, sometimes alliances are formed between companies in the same industry. This is now happening in the furniture industry in northern Europe and the wine industry in Australia and New Zealand. Sometimes companies in different industries combine their strengths to develop new products. Toyota, faced with declining sales in Japan, joined with Toshiba Corporation and Fujitsu Limited to develop a multimedia system for cars, enabling drivers to access the Internet and play computer games on a terminal in the car ("Unjammed," 1998). ABB Asea Brown Boveri, an energy and engineering firm comprising around one thousand companies in more than 140 countries, joined with the Swedish State Railroads in an alliance to design the first-in-the-world train car that serves as an interim office for commuters, with desks, phone hookups, and plug-in modules for laptop computers. Microsoft, as part of an $80 million program to recruit research scientists from around the globe, has established an alliance with a laboratory in Cambridge, England, to draw on resources to which it would not normally have access (Stross, 1997). Toshiba and IBM created a joint venture to develop and manufacture flat-panel liquid-crystal displays, which are used in IBM 750C laptops.

For large and complex global companies with internal operations in many countries, forging alliances between country operations can serve as a source of Positive Turbulence. Pfizer is a good example. Mohand Sidi Said, the president of Pfizer Asia/Africa/Middle East, was driven to find new ways to improve his division's performance. He came up with the idea of organizing his region by size of business and synergy, and not just geography, which had been the traditional structure for many years. He grouped the markets into an association of businesses that were alike in terms of products and size—and only then considered geography.

The newly constituted groups met quarterly in different member countries, not at headquarters. At the beginning of each meeting, the host country gave a best-practices presentation. Because attendees, according to the new grouping, shared certain commonalties, they were able to learn and then apply some of these practices back in their respective countries. And each quarter they learned about a different country's best practices.

These meetings provided an internal forum for Positive Turbulence, engaging the country managers with the accounts of renewal taking place outside their own countries yet still within Pfizer. The cross-fertilization of ideas, the creativity, and the innovation these meetings unleashed was deemed well worth the additional travel and meetings outside corporate headquarters.

Until recently a nation's clout depended largely on its geography and the importance of natural resources developed within its own territories. Knowledge and information were also part of the equation that turned the resources into valuable commodities. Today knowledge and information are even more important. Bringing in those resources from other companies generates synergy and guarantees a constant flow of fresh ideas that can lead to useful innovations.

As Harlan Cleveland eloquently points out in *Birth of a New World* (1993), "It's the countries with the biggest flows of information we call developed. We know that anybody can extract knowledge from the bath of information that nearly drowns us all. You don't have to find it inside your own frontiers, you don't have to grow it in your own soil, you don't have to fabricate it in your own factories or put it together in your own assembly plants. You do [however] have to 'get it all together' in your own brain, and then combine your insight and imagination with other human brain-work in networks, companies, or alliances."

Developing a Supportive Corporate Environment

You can pile up wood in a fireplace and take a match to it, but if there is not enough kindling, it will not ignite. And if the damper is shut down, the fire will never take. If there is no oxygen, it will not burn. If there is too much wind, it will go out. On the other hand, with dry wood piled just right, plenty of kindling, adequate air circulation, and the use of bellows, if necessary, it should light and burn just fine. Turbulence works in similar ways. It must be sur-rounded by a hospitable corporate culture and constantly fed new breaths of life. It is up to a company's senior leadership to make the necessary provisions for doing just this.

We just explored how management can make the best use of the periphery to bring turbulence into an organization. Here we look at ways they can alter the corporate culture so that it does not just receive the turbulence, but welcomes it, learns from it, works with it, grows with it. Some of the ways this can be done are by tak-ing whatever measures are necessary to spark synergy among employees, keeping the focus of the leadership's mission clear, seek-ing ways to perpetuate organizational renewal at every step of the way, and building a strong base of support for Positive Turbulence at the managerial level.

The ideal situation is to develop a corporate culture in which exploration and original thinking are admired, not stifled—even if it occasionally looks as though it is outside the norm. I am suggesting that all managers permit (even encourage) their employees to follow the scent on their own when they detect something intriguing on the periphery. Research verifies that people will put in extra time and effort if they have some freedom to explore intrinsically motivated interests (Amabile, 1996). At first this may require a little faith— faith that the process, the mental chemistry, will take place when intelligent people are given the freedom to follow their own trail.

Sparking Synergy Among Employees

Synergy is that wonderful electrifying energy that comes from combining different elements and entities, whether putting together employees from one company or division with those from another, or putting new information in front of old employees, or simply having the right person in the right place at the right time. Synergy may be a bit like spontaneous combustion, in that the sparks just happen, but within the context of Positive Turbulence, the corporate leadership can help to generate synergy. It can put in place different structures, such as internal trade shows, promote informal information exchanges, and put before employees all kinds of wonderfully novel and even strange ideas.

Holding Internal Trade Shows. Of course it is important to tap into the knowledge and expertise of people outside the organization, but we would be foolish indeed to ignore the talent at home. The bright, clever, maybe even off-the-wall thinkers in our own organization have the potential to perform the same function as outside experts, which is fundamentally this: to trigger the collective synapses.

A core thesis of this book is that the process of renewal begins when you put a new piece of information into the hands of a creative thinker, who will twist it and turn it and eventually make a connection between that new tidbit and the company's mission. That kind of smack-yourself-in-the-forehead connection can be triggered by a colleague as readily as from an outside guest—if only people know what their colleagues are up to. And that is the function of what I am calling corporationwide trade shows. With these internal trade shows, people can learn about what their colleagues in other departments, divisions, and even subsidiary companies are doing in a show-and-tell format. This synergy between employees then becomes a source of Positive Turbulence inside the organization.

The Eastman Worldwide Technical Conference is held each year for all Eastman Chemical Company employees who develop and deploy technology. The four-day event includes informal gatherings for employees to get to know one another, paper and poster sessions, display booths, and a vendor exhibit held on the last day when the doors are open to customers, vendors, and professional societies. The company believes that cross-functional attendees are more likely to stay in touch when they have such face-to-face meetings. Because company security is high, employees can talk to each other there quite openly about their research without fear that the competition will learn about current projects and implied direction.

The advantage of an internal trade show over an external one, such as COMDEX, which I discussed in Chapter Two, is that the information exchanged is in some way related to the company's business, so there is increased opportunity for it to be applicable from one division to another. The advantage of external trade shows is that they may offer much more new information, hence, a greater source of turbulence, though less may be usable. However, what one division does may be so foreign to another that it seems as though it may well have come from the far side of the periphery.

Promoting Informal Information Exchanges. The sharing of information from one employee to another, from one division to the next, can extend the life of one innovation into another area or field or product. This can be done in a number of ways, including by encouraging employees to share information or by creating informal meeting spaces.

Nissan Design International has no departmentally encoded locks, and the designers are encouraged to roam freely through the studios and forage through the notes and sketches of their colleagues. They may make use of ideas that stimulate them, as long as they give them their own spin and acknowledge the source of the inspiration. Because of this style, final designs are usually unattributable since they result from openly shared sketches and ideas. To keep the spark of interest and ideas alive, management at NDI is encouraged to swap people who are working on a particular design, and often in midstream.

Cross-functional information exchanges can be especially valuable to very large organizations, those with separate operating divisions that traditionally have had very little to do with one another. If they are willing to ignore these rigid boundaries and look instead to the potential that lies between business units—what Gary Hamel, visiting professor of strategic management at the London Business School, and C. K. Prahalad, professor at the University of Michigan Business School (1991) once termed the "corporate white space"—they may find a brilliant cross-connection.

Hamel and Prahalad point to Kodak, which in the early 1990s began looking for ways to combine its corporate expertise in chemicals (film and processing) with its knowledge of electronic imaging (copiers) to produce a completely new photographic medium, something that would allow consumers to view and edit their photographs on a television screen and store them safely. We know it now, a few years later, as digital photography.

Creating Informal Meeting Spaces. We have seen how informal meeting spaces in particular can facilitate frequent interactions between and among employees. For Positive Turbulence to thrive in a company, it is often useful to have many such spaces. Pitney Bowes goes a step further. The author of an article for *Fast Company* reported that when he visited the company, he thought he had entered a theme park with cobblestone streets, a town square, and street signs (Kirsner, 1998). Among its meeting spaces Pitney Bowes has a French-style café and a 1950s diner to entice people to come out of their offices and cubicles and interact with each other. Then there are the "friendly hallways, complete with gumball machines," which, according to Matthew Kissner, president and CEO, "foster impromptu conversations. We want people to bump into each other, talk about what they're doing, and exchange information that they wouldn't otherwise exchange."

These meeting spaces have served the company well, with the company's innovations paying off handsomely, and also serving customers well. Peggy Anson, the vice president of human resources, has commented on the healthy sense of restlessness in the organization. And who could wonder, with so many possibilities for exchanging information, reinvigorating thinking, stimulating creativity, and implementing innovation?

Encouraging Free-Ranging Ideas. Throughout this book I have stressed the essential role that multiple perspectives, far-flung information, and wild-and-crazy ideas have in leading to innovation and the importance of exposing employees as much as possible to what is novel and different in an attempt to get them out of the usual groove so that they can approach problems in completely fresh ways.

Remember the story of Weird Al and his at-times detached ideas, an oversight that was fortunately redressed by an astute new manager. Al's story is a true tale, and with a message. It is very likely that you have a Weird Al or Weird Alice somewhere in your organization. Not only should you keep one eye open for this person, but you need to recognize and praise this person publicly for coming up with such an array of ideas. In this way others in the company will see how much broad-ranging ideas are valued. Point out how unusual ideas lead to important developments. This positive reinforcement of the generation of wild ideas will perpetuate this whole process.

Being Open to Off-Center Perspectives. Weird Al has a counterpart in another company, which must also remain anonymous. Like Al, Arnie has an off-center way of looking at the world, but he also has a rather bizarre way of presenting himself. Such strange behavior can be off-putting to others because they do not know how to respond. Yet underneath such strangeness, as you will see in Arnie's story, often lies genius or, at the very least, the seeds of innovation.

Arnie can be found on the barren northwest coast of Scotland in a facility that houses both processing and research for the seaweed used in the production of alginates. Alginates can be found in many food products, where they are used as stabilizers or emulsifiers to, quite literally, hold the food together.

The corporate headquarters of this company is in London. Not long ago, two senior managers were paying a routine visit to the research laboratory. As they made their way through the facility, guided by their host, the research director, the two men witnessed a very curious sight.

Coming toward them down the hall was a man who deliberately bumped into everyone he passed and then spun away, all the while muttering to himself. They could see that the collisions were not random but purposeful: the man clearly went out of his way to bump into people. Before they had time to ask the research director for an explanation, the muttering man walked right into one of the visitors, with a gentle but obvious thud.

"Interesting," the man said softly. "Very interesting." And he continued on his path, bumping into the next person.

The director, accustomed to his researcher's quirky ways, could only apologize to the visitors. "That's Arnie. He's one of our very best. You remember Arnie—the one who solved old 419, and, oh yes, the Chilean project. I'm not sure what he's working on now, but it's bound to be something good. Sorry, sir, again."

After the visit, the director escorted the senior team to the train station and returned to the plant to ask Arnie about his hallway performance.

"Oh, that," Arnie replied, with a grin. "We have a problem with our effluent pipes. I was just trying to find out what it feels like to be a piece of seaweed going down a clogged effluent pipe, bumping up against some lodged particles. Not to worry. I believe I've solved the problem."

Arnie was fortunate to have a boss who understood and valued his unique contribution and the behavioral baggage that often accompanied him on the road to creativity. The company was fortunate to have Arnie—someone who followed his own spirit and made remarkable contributions to the company as well.

Research and development units exist in nearly every industry, ranging from small departments of a few dedicated souls to enormous facilities with several hundred researchers and multi-million-dollar budgets. These R&D units are charged with coming up with the new ideas, new products, and new processes that will keep the company in a healthy competitive position. Their job is to imagine things that no one has envisioned before. We should not be surprised that the people who are best at it have minds that work in different ways from the rest of us.

Many companies, however, are not tolerant of such strange behavior as that demonstrated by Arnie. Others cannot figure out what to do with the myriad ideas tossed out by some highly inventive types such as Al. Yet not only do these "creatives" come up with worthy and welcome solutions, but their very free-ranging style, properly nourished and acknowledged by management, can be infectious, serving as the synergistic spark so necessary to keep Positive Turbulence flowing freely.

Savvy R&D managers recognize that creatives can function only if they have the kind of freedom accorded Arnie and, eventually, Al. These managers understand that they must often serve as a kind of buffer between the "creative types" and the "corporate types." If they are adept at it, both the research staff and the corporation benefit.

Keeping the Focus Clear

As you can imagine, if organizations were filled primarily with Als and Arnies they would probably be very amusing and fascinating places to work, but it is not likely that the real business of the business would get done. That is why organizations have both creative types and corporate types. In this book I have emphasized the role of the creative freethinkers because too often their views are overlooked in the drive for the bottom line. And in a company run by Positive Turbulence, their input is essential.

So although Positive Turbulence depends on a constant churning of information and novel tangential ideas, there must be a counterbalance, which is accomplished by keeping clearly in mind the company's goals and direction. That means taking into account the organization's mission and striking a comfortable and productive balance between idea generation and program implementation.

Not Losing Sight of the Company's Mission. An organization that fully implements Positive Turbulence can be a pretty heady place to work. Outside speakers from all different fields address the employees, followed by animated discussions. Continuous reinvigoration follows from hiring smart, forward-thinking new employees. There are plenty of Als and Arnies who are teaching everyone—through their own modi operandi—how to examine problems while colliding with others in a corridor or standing on their heads or whatever. Retreats, internal trade shows, foreign assignments, and travel opportunities develop employees. Groups throughout the company are given free creative rein, sometimes even with no time limits or expectations.

The outcome can be overwhelming sometimes: too many ideas going off in too many different directions with not enough resources or time to evaluate them all or carry them out. You do not want to discourage initial randomness, because that is where some of the most unexpected solutions may come from. But no organization can afford to go off on wild goose chases after every interesting idea.

Instead, you need to apply those ideas quite specifically to your company's mission statement. Allow adequate time for the ideas to take some shape before you do that, because you do not want to rule out something prematurely or out of course, as Al's ideas were. Farfetched projects may very well be part of your company's mission; sometimes it just takes adequate time to review the projects carefully to discover that they are.

Balancing Idea Generation with Implementation. In a number of companies I know of where Positive Turbulence flourishes, management has set up a system or a procedure for capturing and processing the ideas while freeing the scouts to go back out and pick up more. Although the system can take many forms, the common denominator is that the structure formalizes a link between people who like to have ideas and people who like to implement them.

What I am talking about is balance—balancing the hot minds of implementers with the hot minds of the idea generators. That is the charge for those of us in the innovation business. All people are capable of both originating and implementing to varying degrees, but differences in personality and experience lead some people to be better at generating new ideas and others to be better at ingeniously converting ideas into products or processes that actually work. Together they will accomplish a finished product that makes money for the enterprise. Together they will produce novel and useful ideas that work. The tricky part is not to stymie people by putting them in the wrong place, as Al was when he was sent to the mill to handle problems there, instead of being kept in research. You want your employees engaged and challenged and fulfilled, not stymied or frustrated or thwarted.

Balancing Creativity with Managerial Skills. The nature of managerial work is often incompatible with the nature of creativity, as we saw in Al's case. Creativity requires periods of incubation, great concentration, much freedom, complexity, initiative, a sense of play. Management involves constant activity, dealing with many contacts and separate activities, a structured approach, a search for order and predictability, the ability to react.

Positive Turbulence needs both groups: creative people to fuel and be fueled by the turbulence and managers to direct and control it. Difficulties arise when the right person is put in the wrong track. Often I have seen creative people promoted into management positions for their creativity because the company had no other way to reward their success. In these cases the organization took a double hit. It now had someone with poor management skills in a position that did not call on the person's expertise or creativity.

A far better approach is the bifurcated way to the top known as dual career ladders used in organizations such as Electronic Data Systems (EDS), Georgia-Pacific Corporation, Schering-Plough

Corporation, Read-Rite Corporation, Cisco Systems, Robert Bosch GMBH, International Paper Company, Microsoft, and IBM. Even new companies such as Electronic Arts, a video game designer, has dual career ladders. These parallel career paths are designed to provide a structure of advancement for technical professionals who are not interested in traditional management roles—as well as the traditional path for those who wish to be management candidates. The two career pathways should be comparable in terms of status and compensation but not with regard to task.

Although there needs to be a certain autonomy of each group, there also must be a creative tension, so getting the distance between the two just right is essential. If it is too close, management thinking reduces risk taking and the freedom needed to produce novel ideas. If it is too far away, the novel ideas never find a corporate champion.

Management needs to come up with ways to create or reduce the distance, both psychological and physical, between the two groups. Building links to the decision makers to help gain implementation of the creatives' ideas can reduce the distance, while giving the creatives more free rein can increase it.

Perpetuating Organizational Renewal

Every day organizations are faced with changes all around them—the vicissitudes of the marketplace, changing industry regulations, a competitor's activities, and more. These changes require responses, so the company must develop the ability to respond. In other words, leaders must manage the change before it manages them.

By giving employees challenges and creating a certain disequilibrium through introducing the unexpected, the untried, even the disquieting in many different manifestations, employees stay alert. And when they are on their metaphorical toes, like a tennis player waiting for the next serve, they are able to move with and find new ways to respond to the changes. Without that flexibility, they are unable to find their way through unpredictable situations.

With it, they can, and this keeps the organization in a perpetual state of renewal.

The creative leader sees organizational renewal as critically necessary and is willing to lead the company through the turbulent waters with the belief that when the process is over, the organization will be in a better position to serve the marketplace. To engage deliberately in such risk taking along with the discomfort of change while still keeping an eye on the future perfect state is a good test of a creative leader's mettle.

To initiate renewal, leaders in concert with the normal flow of doing things take on exploration and discovery and, with it, risk. Constantly embracing the unknown would make most people crazy; the kind of leader required to stand at the helm of an organization driven by Positive Turbulence thrives on it. Newness, along with its complexities and uncertainties, attracts, rather than deters, these individuals.

All of us would agree intellectually that some risk is needed to secure a lifeline to the future, but it is the savvy, creative leader who actually welcomes and opens the door to it. Then, along with the courage to engage risk, the leader also needs the courage to hold steady even when there is no immediate, dramatic payback. Creative leaders are able to do this because they know that renewal is not always an even course, and they are confident that embracing changes, engaging risk, and welcoming creativity in all its weird and wonderful forms, leads to innovation and then to renewal.

Keeping Turbulence Positive

Turbulence by its nature is a variable force, with the ever-present potential for it to turn negative. Skillful, knowledgeable, astute leadership can make the difference between turbulence being negative or positive. Effectively managing a turbulence-driven organization requires a little of Leonardo da Vinci's passion for creativity and innovation, Socrates' method of systematic doubt and questioning, Nelson Mandela's patience and conviction, Nostradamus's ability to foresee the future, Amelia Earhart's fearlessness in risk taking, and Shakespeare's knowledge of human nature.

Although a number of leaders do possess differing degrees of skills from that impressive list, others may not. Yet there are still certain steps they can take to ensure that the turbulence they shepherd into their organizations remains positive: steer clear of gratuitous turbulence, test the waters to gauge the effect of the turbulence, keep sensors attuned to the needs of customers and the opportunities presented by crises, and devise alternative action plans that take into account future eventualities.

Avoiding Gratuitous Turbulence

Throughout this book we have examined quite thoroughly the process by which companies deliberately search out the faint signals of new trends and bring them inside the organization to serve as the raw material for creativity. It is surely apparent how profoundly I admire and honor pure creativity in all its multiple, wondrous forms. But let us not get carried away. Creativity is not an end unto itself—at least not in the hard world of business.

Overinfatuation with turbulence can cause just as much damage as its obverse. When Positive Turbulence becomes the be-all and end-all, management risks damaging its credibility with employees. When each first whiff of a new opportunity *always* starts wheels spinning and sparks flying, the organization is in danger of becoming addicted to the adrenaline rush of change. In such a giddy atmosphere, established strategy and agreed-on goals are too easily and too casually discarded. This sort of knee-jerk creativity is extremely hard on in-place systems, and it usually has extremely negative results.

What is needed is the moderating impact of a courageous and creative leader with the skills to control the flow of turbulence and direct it to useful ends. The leader needs the backup of a supportive corporate environment and established structures for translating the turbulence into a working asset. If the structures

and the right environment are not in place, the leader's early task
is to create them.

Testing the Waters

Many organizations have rigid structures that have served the
employees for many years. If you rattle the walls too suddenly or too
strongly, you may lose the employees' respect and your ability to
lead. If all of your praise goes to the Als and Arnies, you risk losing
the goodwill of steady, loyal employees who have more linear styles
of thinking and working.

Implementing the move toward a Positive Turbulence–driven
organization is best done gradually, monitoring the results at each
stage of the way to see if it is creating novelty or debilitating confusion, innovation or paralysis. The aim, as we know, is to keep the
turbulence at just the right intensity—enough to get the employees stimulated and challenged and moving ahead in new ways, yet
not so much that it stuns them into inaction.

At the Center for Creative Leadership we learned this lesson
during our early days. David P. Campbell, who later became the
executive vice president of the center, was working with a group of
managers from a major consumer products company. The assembled
group represented various business segments of the company, which
was known for its rigid structure. Each separate business unit was a
tightly organized fiefdom, and most of those present in our classroom
that day had never even met their counterparts in other units.

Campbell gamely tried to get them to participate in a series of
exercises designed to jolt people from their familiar and safe mind-
sets. Most of the participants sat stiffly, now and then glancing over
at their boss, trying to figure out why he had brought them to this
place and inflicted this amazing speaker on them.

Afterward Campbell confessed that this was the most difficult
audience he had ever encountered. The real problem was that the
new ideas were coming too fast for the participants; they had never
done anything like this. The company had taken a risk in trying
something new. Unfortunately, in this company there was not an

existing precedent for, to make an analogy, taking hockey players to a ballet recital.

This experience illustrates that the concepts of Positive Turbulence are not a simplistic formula for speaking creativity and innovation. Too much new and different information for the participants can easily lead to someone's concluding, "We tried Positive Turbulence once, and it didn't work." By constantly monitoring how the turbulence is being received into the culture of the organization, with mechanisms in place for doing so, you help keep the ship on an even keel.

Tuning In to Customers and Clients

In addition to testing the waters of turbulence, it is important to stay attuned to the responses it generates among the outside groups—usually customers and clients—your company deals with. Because of the fervor of Positive Turbulence, it is easy to become so caught up in the novelty of a new product or service that managers overlook how their customers or clients may respond to it. By truly listening to customers, especially in their own settings, you can use the information they give you to determine direction, uncover opportunities, motivate the product development team, and stimulate creative thinking.

The type of listening I am talking about here goes beyond just the findings of market research. This listening, in either the home or workplace of the customer or client, supplements and energizes the statistical data and links the actions of a product developer directly with the needs of the end user.

Today's smart organizations are finding all sorts of ways to pick up on what their customers are saying. Following are just a few examples. What they all have in common is that they involve direct, and often interactive, engagement with consumers.

- Before designing their book retrieval software, Lotus engineers spent time in public libraries, observing how children handled books.

- Yamaha Corporation has established a center for its latest music-making technology in the heart of London, where Europe's young and talented musicians can drop by and experiment with alternative technology for making the music of the future, and in the process give the company designers and marketers immediate feedback.

- Toyota provided CAD/CAM machines for customers to design their own dream cars, which allowed the Toyota engineers to see the possibilities their customers imagined.

- To determine what the customer expected in the design of its new automobiles, Volvo used a rather sophisticated form of data collection, called "softnomic data," which assessed the more qualitative responses of their customer base.

- Mazda Motor Corporation funded a subsidiary company under the control of the R&D division that provided a mechanism by which customers could talk directly with senior design staff.

- Designers of Wrangler jeans, produced by VF Corporation, visited Tokyo parks to observe what the young people were wearing on Sunday afternoon outings to gather ideas for future fashion and products.

The process of watching consumers use products and services in situ has been called "empathic design" by Harvard Business School professors Dorothy Leonard and Jeffrey Rayport (1997). At issue is what a customer does with a product, not what the designers or engineers intended for it. Leonard and Rayport recommend that observers include those who are skilled in behavioral observation as well as those who understand the organizational capabilities of the design team.

Some companies—IBM, Xerox Corporation, Hewlett-Packard Company, and Motorola, for example—hire social scientists to observe customers using products. Some hire anthropologists, ethnographers, and psychologists. The information that the observers take away with them can be categorized as coming from the periphery, and thus a source of turbulence; properly ushered in to the organization, it can be a positive force for change.

The success of an article testifies to the validity of its message, as we see in the case of Theodore Levitt's (1975) retrospective to "Marketing Myopia," in which he suggested consulting clients to identify gaps in the service or products offered. Note that Levitt did not suppose that the clients would give detailed specifications for the service or product they wanted, though sometimes that happens. Rather, the client, if gently encouraged, can describe an outcome or a product that would be beneficial. The organization can then ask R&D or product development, "Can you design a process that will deliver outcome X to clients?" or "Can we make a product that's like our product Y but has the following characteristics?"

Learning from Crises

No sane person would suggest deliberately engineering a crisis as a way of stimulating creative thinking, but the unfortunate fact is that crises do occur, and they do have to be dealt with. When a crisis hits an organization that already has a creative climate, it is often the catalyst for significant innovation.

When things are going swimmingly, the tendency is to leave well enough alone. But when trouble erupts, decisions must be faced, and out of the responses come new directions, new lessons. At the end of 1998, as this book is being written, corporations are facing some of the biggest crises many of them have ever had to face—forfeited loans from foreign countries, plunging stock prices worldwide, devastating economies in countries around the globe. All of this will have severe impact. Yet through this crisis, companies presumably will discover new ways to do business, new ways to stay on top of a changing marketplace, new ways to weather a rough financial sea. The more innovative their responses are, the more easily they will be able to deal with subsequent crises. Without this upheaval, with their bottom lines rising or holding steady, they most likely would not have undertaken major changes.

Planning for Eventualities

While the information coming in from the periphery may be random, unknown, and even capricious, and the chaos it stirs up often unforeseen, leaders can never leave the consequences wholly up to fate. Instead they need to look at trends that are out on the horizon and see if they can get an inkling as to what might be headed their way. They also need to devise some plan that sets up structures for dealing with future scenarios, and they need to establish a firm base of support from among the managerial sector.

Projecting Future Scenarios.   By far the most substantive, most sophisticated mechanism for capturing trends and putting them to constructive use is scenario planning. It is similar to strategic planning, but uses much wider lenses and looks at the world from multiple perspectives.

In general terms, scenario planning brings together creative leaders and thought leaders from several fields and captures their ideas on upcoming trends. Projections are then made on what the future will look like, given those trends, and the projections are expressed in the form of written scenarios.

For organizations, the end product of the planning process is a large document that lays out these scenarios and suggests several possible courses of action. In effect, the organizations' leaders are left with a guidebook to the future. When a new trend manifests itself, they can review the section of the document that describes it and find recommendations for their best action. Because the scenario has already been envisioned and appropriate responses already thought through, they are not caught by surprise.

In the minds of many of us, scenario planning is linked closely with a company that pioneered its use—Royal Dutch/Shell Group—and in fact with one remarkable individual—Arie de Geus, a member of the corporate planning staff responsible for putting scenario planning in place. De Geus believes that companies can use scenarios to move ahead of the competition and that this affords them "the only sustainable competitive advantage in an environment of rapid innovation and change" (de Geus, 1997). De Geus is also credited with originating the concept of the learning organization—one in which the whole organization accomplishes the learning. Learning organizations are able to turn information into knowledge and increase the organization's capacity to renew itself—to learn.

The Royal Dutch/Shell experience has been described by de Geus himself, in *The Living Company: Habits for Survival in a Turbulent Business Environment* (1997), and by Peter Schwartz, in *The Art of the Long View* (1991). Schwartz points out that Royal Dutch/Shell uses five wide lenses—society, environment, economics, technology, and politics—to view the horizon, and that these lenses serve as frameworks within which to organize what is observed. In several key areas, then, the company's executives have advance analysis of probable future events and both the long-term and short-term impact of those events on the company, its various businesses, suppliers, and markets. The stated purpose of this scenario-building activity is to provide senior management at Royal Dutch/Shell with insights and perspectives before they read about them in *The Economist*.

Here is a simple example of applying the five lenses to the situation at Shell so you can see how scenario planning works. The economic picture showed an increasing need to cut costs. A review of environmental concerns (the lens of political climate) revealed increasing demands to reduce pollution. These factors together indicated that the development of more fuel-efficient jet engines would be likely. Royal Dutch/Shell then needed to explore the potential impact of a move to more efficient engines on a company that produces and markets jet fuel, and it needed to assess how demand would be affected over the next ten to fifteen years. The more efficient engine suggested to Royal Dutch/Shell that it should begin thinking about a future scenario that would involve having the company reduce drilling, pumping, or refining oil or having it look for alternative sources for the fuel.

Looking through the lens of population figures, Royal Dutch/ Shell would want to know how population changes will affect the company. One major upcoming change is that an enormous sector—baby boomers—is moving into its senior years. Will they be flying more or less? Have more or less money to spend on airfares? What about the impact of 2 billion teenagers in the year 2001, when, for the first time in modern history, young people will make up half the world's population (Schwartz, 1991)? Will teleconferencing developments (the technology development lens) mean that people will be traveling more or less in the future?

Royal Dutch/Shell has added to its scenario planning a factor that ensures that the process will always result in a fresh perspective: the director of strategic planning, who oversees the scenario planning process, is limited to a term of three years. And every other term, the person tapped to fill that role comes from outside the company (I have noted often in this book the value of an outsider's perspective). In this way, the company guarantees that entrenched culture and long-standing biases will not color this critical planning process.

A number of companies bring in outside strategic planners. One firm they use is IdeaScope Associates, a Boston/San Francisco–based management consulting company specializing in strategic innovation. The company uses a process it calls Thought Leader Visioning Methodology, which involves using a panel of outside experts to stimulate the thinking of their clients. This methodology was developed based on one of IdeaScope's core philosophies: "Visionary companies are seldom those that only talk to themselves." Thought leaders for the panel are selected to represent the trends that will shape the future.

Setting Up Channels for Overseeing Positive Turbulence. As far as I know, no company has a director of Positive Turbulence or an Office of Positive Turbulence—yet. However, there needs to be some forum or vehicle through which managers at all levels can discuss and get feedback on the process of Positive Turbulence. There also needs to be some way they can get help evaluating the whole process: the lessons learned, the knowledge gained, and the ideas developed therefrom.

The first thing to do toward this end is to encourage people to communicate the new ideas and new information they find. Give them a protocol or, better still, an individual or office to report to. Set up organizational machinery to interpret the changes sensed on the periphery and do an initial evaluation. Establish credibility for this machinery. Assign a group of higher-level people who will meet periodically to review the initial evaluations and ask for additional information if the report is not self-explanatory. The logical time to do this in mature industries is at the regular periodic reviews and budget planning sessions. However, it is also important to set up a special channel that can expedite the process and respond quickly to an opportunity. You might also establish an internal procedure to feed the recommendations to the people charged with steering the ship, finding the funds, and tweaking the policy.

Solidifying Managerial Support for Positive Turbulence. When the leaders at the top of an organization endorse the concepts of Positive Turbulence, we can reasonably assume that the organization will have the kind of environment in which it flourishes. But it would be naive to suppose that all managers share the leader's enthusiasm for rich chaos; resistance to change shows itself at all levels and in all departments. What is needed is an effort, probably spearheaded by the senior leadership, to enlist the participation of line managers.

Top management needs to establish a climate supportive of Positive Turbulence. They can do this by making public statements in support of all aspects of Positive Turbulence, promoting the idea that innovation is everyone's business, and helping to create an atmosphere that encourages thinking and the communication of ideas.

Human resource departments can play a key role too. They need to recognize that creative people are sufficiently different from those less creative and that they should not exclude them from hiring procedures. Human resources should include creativity and innovation as categories in performance reviews and help evaluate potential business acquisitions by analyzing how much creativity such a merger would contribute to the company.

Establishing free and open lines of communication is also essential. Some of the ways this can be done is by setting up a company intranet, creating a clearinghouse for innovative ideas, establishing an information center for storing fringe data, promoting formal exchanges of ideas across groups, and cross-pollinating ideas through rotating people and roles.

Professional consciousness raising is important in helping to strengthen managerial support for Positive Turbulence. This might involve holding in-house conferences on different aspects of Positive Turbulence; encouraging managers to attend professional meetings, join societies, and return to universities to stay in touch with the state of the art; and promoting direct contact between senior people and their counterparts in potential customer organizations.

A few successes of the sort documented in this book go a long way toward reinforcing faith in Positive Turbulence and overcoming resistance to it. Organizationally, however, we have a long way to go. I wonder how many companies would permit an employee like Arnie to walk down a corridor colliding into others because such action was part of his problem-solving process, or how many companies would allow a manager to bring in an ornithologist to talk to the research scientists about humpback whales singing to each other, let alone defend such actions to a budget committee.

———

In this chapter we have looked at what it takes to welcome, cultivate, and nourish turbulence in an organization and have seen from a number of real-life examples how to control this extraordinary force and manage the people who will work with it on a daily basis. We have seen a few examples of what happens when it is done well and when it is done not so well. Finally, we will look in depth at three companies that have used Positive Turbulence in a variety of ways and learned how to use it, and we see the benefits that have accrued to their companies as a consequence.

Chapter Six

Positive Turbulence in Action

To understand any process, it is often necessary to break it down into its component parts and look at each of those parts from a variety of angles. And so thus far we have examined the dynamics of Positive Turbulence, what a supportive base for it looks like, how the ideal group for developing Positive Turbulence would function, and what it takes to manage a Positive Turbulence–driven company effectively.

What is missing from this portrait so far is the whole picture. So in this chapter we see Positive Turbulence in action, in all its wonderful manifestations. To give a sense of the whole picture, we look at three very different companies: Norfolk Southern, a railroad formed by the merger of conservative Norfolk and Western Railway Company with the innovative Southern Railway System; Hallmark, a communications company known for its greeting cards and outstanding television programs; and 3M, a manufacturer of pressure-sensitive tapes, sandpaper, fabric protectors, and repositionable notes, among other products.

Although in some cases the dynamics of Positive Turbulence were consciously adopted by these companies, in others they were not. And although the companies go about their pursuit of turbulence in very different ways, they share a common outcome: continuous renewal.

Moving Forward at Norfolk Southern

Today Norfolk Southern is a highly successful and profitable company, with generated sales in 1997 of more than $4 billion and a one-year sales growth of 11.5 percent. It has more than twenty-five thousand employees and a market value estimated at over $11.5 billion. The absorption of more than half of Conrail in 1999 will give the railroad some twenty-one thousand miles of routes in twenty-two states (mostly east of the Mississippi River) and into Ontario, Canada. But to get the full picture, it is necessary to take a brief look at some history.

When railroads first began crisscrossing the United States in the nineteenth century, they were the ideal form of transportation: fast, inexpensive, solid, flexible, and expansive. Then along came cars, trucks, and airplanes, and the industry declined. Theodore Levitt (1975) attributed that decline to the railroads' inability to see themselves as being in the transportation business rather than just the railroad business; they were railroad-centered rather than transportation-oriented, product-focused instead of customer-oriented. The result of such a narrow-framed definition was that the railroads did not envision alternative transportation services.

You could also say the railroads' near demise was due as well to their having failed to pay attention to the periphery. Information coming from beyond the industry would undoubtedly have suggested the changes coming along so they could have responded to them in a proactive rather than reactive way.

Before the merger in 1982, according to Joe Gelmini, currently director of workforce development for the merged Norfolk Southern, Southern Railway was blessed with two forward-looking leaders. The first was Bill Brosnan: "He was a person who challenged every single individual at the railroad to constantly look for new ways to do things. He stretched people to their limits; he had people doing things that even they didn't think they could do. He was a man who would give great rewards to people who came through with projects that worked. On the other hand, he was also a person who could come down very hard on people—not so much if they failed, but if they didn't try or if they didn't give their all to accomplish what he thought they could."

After Brosnan came Graham Claytor. Gelmini calls him a "very innovative guy who had a totally different personality and a totally different way of working with people—much more team-oriented and participative. He believed in seeking input from a variety of sources before making a decision. Mr. Claytor would seek out all the ideas and opinions and then try to synthesize the information."

It was Graham Claytor's brother, Robert, who worked for the Norfolk and Western, who helped forge the merger. One of the most successful mergers in the transportation industry—perhaps in any industry—it brought together two proud transportation companies that had competed with each other (in some cases over the same track) in a very dramatic coupling.

Each railroad had its own culture and way of doing business that was determined by the markets it served. The Norfolk and Western was dominated by the coal industry and the transportation of coal from the mountains to the coast. Having improved on and stayed with steam technology much longer than the other railroads, the Norfolk and Western consequently became the leading builder of steam locomotive power in this country and perhaps in the world.

The Southern Railway operated from the beginning in multiple markets and focused on a broader market mix of commodities. So while the Norfolk and Western stayed with and improved on the basic mode of transportation—the steam engine, which was adequate for its single-product needs—the Southern Railway had to adapt to broader and changing demands. The Southern Railway was the first to dieselize its locomotive fleet completely in the late 1940s and early 1950s. It led the way in mechanization of track maintenance equipment and also in automated computerized hump yards, and it developed the all-door boxcar, the Big John grain hoppers, and other specialized types of freight equipment that could move materials for customers that trucks could not do at all or could only do less efficiently and less cheaply. "There was a history of innovation by solving problems through different ways of thinking," explains Gelmini. "This thinking was a part of the history of the Southern."

The merger brought together two companies with very different backgrounds and approaches. The Norfolk and Western was the adaptively creative, more conservative organization, and Southern Railway was the innovatively creative organization. The Norfolk and Western wanted to improve and make processes better, whereas the Southern was more open to doing things differently and in new ways.

During the early years of the Center for Creative Leadership's relationship with the railroads, which began nearly twenty years ago, we helped them resolve those different styles so they could work together productively, and we helped them incorporate the practices of Positive Turbulence into their company culture.

Today Norfolk Southern is a revitalized company, thanks in large part to its having adopted the basic principles of Positive Turbulence. It pays careful attention to the periphery, it encourages cross-fertilization at all levels, it actively promotes receptivity to Positive Turbulence, and it looks at change as a great source for ongoing renewal.

Paying Attention to the Periphery

Perhaps through learning the lessons from its forebears, Norfolk Southern came to recognize how important the information coming in from the periphery can be and how essential it is to make use of it. And so the railroad looks at what other industries are doing and how they are doing it, and it takes advantage of what outside reading can reveal.

Looking Outside the Industry. The notion of looking outside the railroad industry "was internalized in a lot of Norfolk Southern managers," according to Gelmini. "Forget about what your competition is doing, but look at who does it best regardless of the industry."

Before establishing its national customer service center in 1992, Norfolk Southern benchmarked several customer service centers, including the American Express Company. "We wanted to see how American Express organized and how they trained their people for customer service," says Gelmini. The railroad also benchmarked Duke Power Company's centralized customer service center in Charlotte: "We paid attention to the lessons from those customer service centers. We also visited CSX and Conrail to observe a railroad perspective, but we obtained more useful information from the two nonrailroad groups. We patterned much of what we did from those visits."

Although it had a good safety record, Norfolk Southern nevertheless wanted to improve it. "The first thing we looked at," says Gelmini, "was who had the best safety record—in any industry. And we found that one of the leaders in safety was the DuPont Corporation. Having started back in the 1800s as a company that made gunpowder, they had an extraordinary focus on safety that became part of their culture. So we spent a lot of time with DuPont. We finally entered a contractual agreement with them to actually pay them to come on our property and do a safety assessment. As a result of that, they gave us a lot of ideas, and they ran some training for us and our supervisors."

Still, Norfolk Southern had to adapt many of the practices to its own application. Gelmini recalls, "We had to make some modifications because the nature of the railroad is that we are spread out over large geographic areas; we don't have plants or factories where there are large concentrations of people that you can work with. On the railroad you have crews operating twenty-four hours a day, rather independently."

Just as safety had become "part of DuPont's culture," it became part of Norfolk Southern's. "Training has played an important role," says Gelmini, "but mostly it's been people working at a grassroots level with each other having safety huddles. It is a mind-set. Safety has evolved to the way we do business. We would not even think about doing something that wasn't safe."

As to how well Norfolk Southern picked up what it had learned about safety from an outside company, Gelmini proudly reports, "In 1989 we won the Harriman Gold Award for being the safest Class One railroad in the country, and we've won that award every year since. We have achieved safety levels that just a couple of years ago people thought were unattainable in the railroad industry with its inherent hazards." But the company has a goal: "to become the safest transportation company in the world."

When Norfolk Southern wanted to know how it could increase its business with Ford Motor Company, its largest customer, whose cars the railroad transported from assembly line to dealerships all across the country, it again looked outside the industry—in this case, to Federal Express and its "mixing centers."

According to Gelmini, "Ford had kind of a logistics problem, because they would have to park all these automobiles out in some big lot near the assembly plant. It would take them a lot of time to try to get vehicles that were all going to the same place and put them on a railcar." So Norfolk Southern looked at how Federal Express had solved this problem. This is what Gelmini found:

> They hub everything to Memphis and mix it up there, remix it, and then send it back out to the destinations. The story used to be that even if you were shipping something by Federal Express across the street, it would go to Memphis, then it would come back the next day.
>
> So we told Ford, "We'll put in these four mixing centers." They are strategically located around the United States depending on where the plants are. Anything that comes off—and it doesn't matter if it's a truck or Ford Escort—when it comes off the assembly line they just load it on the railcars and those railcars go as a solid train to the mixing center. When they get to the mixing center, we say something like, "Okay, these eighteen vehicles are all going to Greensboro, North Carolina, so we are going to put them on this car and head them that way."

Reading Outside the Field. In Chapter Three I discussed the importance of reading outside the field as another way to tap into the periphery. Here is a story about the innovative solution that came about because an employee was following articles in his local newspaper about the municipal trash dump filling up in Roanoke, Virginia, where he lived.

"There were environmental problems, and nobody wanted to have a trash dump in their backyard," explains Gelmini. "The staff member figured there had to be a way to solve this problem and make some money for the company." Norfolk Southern came up with the idea for Wasteline Express.

"Garbage is now picked up by truck from homes and brought to a central treatment plant in downtown Roanoke, where it is shredded, treated and baled, and loaded into special railcars that were specifically designed and are only used for this particular service. Then it is moved about twenty miles to a special landfill site outside Roanoke. That system took about two years to put into place. It's been a very good business for us, and we are working with several other municipalities to develop a similar scheme for them."

Encouraging Cross-Fertilization

Cross-fertilization is a way to generate Positive Turbulence by bringing together different entities or situations, whether employees from one division into another or a new company into the corporation, all with a view to seeing what novel changes can ensue as a consequence. Although it is a somewhat narrowly focused operation, Norfolk Southern encourages cross-fertilization by moving employees into other roles and other areas of the company and by creating alliances with other companies.

Moving Employees into Other Roles. This process of formally moving employees around began during the time of the merger. It started with the vice presidents of operations for each railroad, who switched jobs so they could learn about the former competitor's operations from a new perspective and ask the "dumb" questions that can only be phrased and asked by an outsider.

Gelmini says that the role switch worked very well:

> It gave each of the vice presidents a good feel for both sides—the two operations as well as the two groups of people. It was so successful, in

fact, that we did it at a number of lower levels, in several different areas of the company—mostly the Operations, Marketing, and Information Technology departments. We moved people who had grown up on one property to a whole different geographic area, away from their normal support system of friends and networks, and threw them into an arena where they very quickly had to learn a new operation, work with different people, and also bring the ideas from their old operation. In effect they were saying, "Here's the way we did it in my last job. Is that the way you guys do it here, and have you ever thought about doing it this way? Or does your way make more sense?"

On a fairly wide basis, we specifically moved people and swapped them around, and it really seemed to facilitate blending the two companies into a new team. Although the railroad operates rather consistently across the tracks, there were different operation idiosyncrasies from one terminal to the next and from one set of geography to the next. As you moved to different parts of the railroad operation, it became quite different, and along came different challenges. There was a great advantage to early and frequent moves. There was a benefit from understanding and developing the knowledge of the job and a feel for the job and an ability to do the job.

Changing jobs promoted an interconnectedness, another aspect of Positive Turbulence, because as employees moved around, they developed new networks of colleagues. They were also able to get a better understanding of the big picture of the company.

Learning About Other Areas of the Company. Sometimes it did not make sense for employees to change locations. Still wanting them to gain a better understanding of other areas and of the company as a whole, Norfolk Southern created opportunities for employees to learn more about the company and its operations.

Gelmini explains that "the railroad always encouraged you to be out on the railroad—between the rails as they used to say. Get out with the crews, get out with the maintenance people and spend time with them and listen to them and find out things from their perspective. Everyone is required to get out and ride trains occasionally and to try to get an understanding of what the business is like at the grassroots level—what is really required to move freight from one place to another."

There was a bonus to these excursions: "We either rode trains or we drove. A lot of times that would force you to be with one or two other people in an automobile for two or three hours at a time. There wasn't a lot to do other than talk about the railroad or tell stories. You were constantly hearing how people did things, and, of course, these people worked all over the railroad and they knew how things were handled in a lot of places. The stories would be heard by the younger folks."

In a sense, these trips were mini-retreats: "We were in a car with each other—no phones, no distractions. Talking with a seasoned railroad person for a few hours was a nice opportunity that doesn't always occur in the busy world of work."

Recognizing the importance of learning about other areas of the company, Norfolk Southern encourages employees to teach others about their particular area of operation. Explains Gelmini, "We were put into roles, particularly in an area that you might not feel real comfortable, and were asked to teach that content to somebody else. At an early age I was thrown into teaching classes on operating rules."

Here too there was an added perk: the teachers learned a lot as well. Gelmini says, "My complaint about teaching at such an early age was that I didn't feel like I knew enough about the subject to teach others. My boss at the time said, 'Well, you will.' I thought he was making a big mistake picking me, but as I look back on it now, he knew if you were going to learn something yourself, then the way to do that was to be responsible for teaching it to others. That happens a lot at Norfolk Southern: younger people are asked to give presentations or classes on some technical aspect of the business, which requires that they prepare and learn about it themselves."

Forging Alliances. The cross-fertilization at Norfolk Southern took on a deeper dimension when the railroad acquired a trucking company, as Gelmini explains:

> We're in the business of moving freight for our customers. We kept hearing from them how much they liked truck service for some kinds of freight on some routes. So we thought maybe we needed to start thinking like truckers rather than railroaders, and we thought a good way to do that was to buy a well-respected trucking line and learn from them. So in 1985 Norfolk Southern bought North American Van Lines, and we took some of the people from the trucking line and put them in charge of our intermodal operations at the railroad.
>
> This resulted in a lot of innovative ideas coming into the railroad. And the upshot of it was we invested in an entirely new kind of equipment, called the RoadRailer®. With all these truck people around, we got to thinking, why do you have to have a container or a trailer that sits on top of a railroad car? Why can't you have a piece of equipment that could operate either on the highway or the railroad?
>
> And eventually we came up with one. It's a fairly conventional-looking trailer, up to fifty feet long, that can be equipped with both highway wheels and railroad wheels. You can drive it like a regular truck trailer, or hook it up to a locomotive and it becomes another train car. So we can move freight all on the highway, or all on the rails, or some combination, whichever makes the most sense for any customer. It's become a big part of our business, and right now we are the only railroad doing it on a large scale.

Engendering Intensity of Turbulence

We saw in Chapter Four the importance of intensity in creating turbulence. Whether through using deadlines, encouraging multiple perspectives, or promoting interactions among employees, Norfolk Southern is able to keep intensity at a peak—though not debilitating—level so that the company can move along on the road to renewal.

Using Deadlines. Urgent deadlines and critical needs can catapult a group into action. Gelmini had been with the railroad a few months in 1969 when Hurricane Camille laid waste to hundreds of miles in and around Charlottesville, Virginia, destroying much railroad property, including a key bridge in the railroad's north-south route, bringing the main line between Atlanta and Washington, D.C., to a standstill.

Gelmini got a call from management. "Pack as many clothes as you can and get to Charlottesville," they told him. "You're going to learn railroading from the ground up." When he got there, he says, "The ground wasn't even there; it had all been washed away. All that was left of the stone arch bridge that carried the main line over the Tye River were four strands of rail spanning this chasm, which was more than a quarter-mile wide."

Gelmini was one of six management trainees the company sent. They frequently worked sixteen to eighteen hours a day. The Southern decided not to rebuild a double-track stone bridge, like the one that had been destroyed, but a substantial single-track steel structure a quarter-mile long, 120 feet above the river. Then they had to figure out the logistics on how to get the steel and the machinery in, since most of the roads had been washed out.

"To this day," says Gelmini, "I'm not sure how we pulled it off, but three weeks to the day after the old stone bridge fell, the first train ran over that new steel bridge. At the time we didn't think much of it, but as I look back on it, it was a unique opportunity to learn what the company is really about. The efforts that it took, the gargantuan hours that people worked—it was plain that those people would do anything to keep the trains running. When people come together for those long hours, thirty-six to forty hours without sleeping, it just cements the idea that the business is the business, and whatever it takes to keep the trains running is what we're going to do."

There are some additional lessons in this story. In it we also see how astute managers using an ad hoc team, effective problem-solving techniques that employ some of the methods of Targeted Innovation, and the introduction of fresh perspectives resulted in a near-miraculous resolution of a crisis.

"Every day," says Gelmini, "the chief engineer would invite all of us to come down to the office at six in the morning and have breakfast together. We would sit around this table with the chief bridge engineer and the chief track engineer, and try to figure out the quickest way to get this bridge rebuilt. They were literally designing the bridge on the tablecloth and the napkins there at the breakfast table."

He continues, "The amazing thing about it for us was being allowed into that inner sanctum, watching the thinking that was going on. They would even ask our opinions, people who were fresh out of college with a couple of months on the job. 'What do you think of this idea?' 'Will this work?' 'What kind of a gusset plate should we use here?' Interestingly, all of us trainees but one are still with the railroad nearly thirty years later."

Gelmini learned a great deal from the experience, and so did the company: "We learned that people were better prepared than we thought, and that good managers can contribute effectively in areas even when they are not technical experts. Since that time, we have been more systematic in moving people between departments to broaden their knowledge of operations and give them the big-picture perspective."

Inviting Multiple Perspectives. By bringing in views from different people in different divisions to focus on a particular problem, companies are able to generate the kind of intensity that can lead to a solution more innovative than probably one viewpoint would be able to provide. Take the example of Norfolk Southern's development of the COLTainer®, an offshoot of the RoadRailer.

Because the RoadRailer operates over both highway and track, it has to adhere to restrictions of both. Highways have weight restrictions, for example. "Most of the things you move on this equipment are fairly lightweight—they bulk out before they weigh out," says Gelmini. This posed a problem for moving a heavy-bulk commodity like coal. So Norfolk Southern came up with a smaller-scale version of a RoadRailer, called the COLTainer®, specifically meant to service an operation where coal was being moved entirely by truck from a coal mine in Alabama to a power plant. Gelmini continues:

> The distance the coal was moving was only seventeen miles, a relatively short distance. So to invest a lot of money in conventional rail equipment to do this made it impractical. But the COLTainer® can move about half the distance on existing rails and then truck the rest of the way to the power plant. So we avoided the cost and environmental disruption of having to build new rail lines.
>
> One of our folks in the Marketing Group was convinced there was a way to get this business for the railroad. He had the idea; then he was given a limited budget and basically a lot of encouragement to see if he could develop the business. He had a lot of cooperation from almost every department in the railroad—certainly the operations department and the mechanical department, which built the railcar. They worked both internally within the railroad and externally. They worked with the public service commission in Alabama. They worked with the environmental people. We had our mechanical department build the prototype equipment and we also had good cooperation from our unions on how the crews were assigned. It was a synergistic process that took about a year and a half.

Encouraging Exchanges. Although the organization stretches across many states, Norfolk Southern depends on frequent exchanges among employees. "Interestingly enough," says Gelmini,

> the railroads also had very well-developed telephonic communication systems even back in the 1950s, before e-mail, pagers, and good radio transmission. I guess the railroads, since the organization is spread out

and depends on people having common understandings, needed to develop their own internal telephone communication systems.

We had frequent and extremely reliable ways to talk with each other. Even by phone we could communicate throughout the system at relatively no cost. The telephonic system was internal, and it allowed us to network. We could talk to people, find out many things—everything from scuttlebutt to needed real information.

As technology has advanced communication so dramatically, Norfolk Southern has implemented many systems for keeping employee exchanges and interactions efficient and frequent. These include extensive use of e-mail, videoconferencing, and continued use of one of the largest privately owned microwave communications networks in the world.

Keeping Turbulence Positive

Because turbulence is volatile, there is always the chance, as we have seen in previous chapters, that it can turn negative. But like other organizations that use turbulence productively, Norfolk Southern has taken steps to ensure that the turbulence remains positive. This includes controlling the turbulence, using Targeted Innovation, and not losing sight of the mission.

Controlling Intensity. Any massive move, such as a merger, can open the throttle to uncontrollable speed. It takes careful management, deliberate preplanning, and diligent oversight to keep the results from derailing the whole operation, which is what Norfolk Southern did. As Gelmini explains, "We didn't miss a beat with the merger. The company grew, and it grew by every measure of efficiency; we improved our safety record, our record of customer satisfaction, and our profits during those five years."

The merger was handled very deliberately. "There wasn't any rush to take premature advantage of cost savings by cutting back people or cutting back service." And a merger team was put into place. "The team was very deliberately constructed. There was a balance between people who had previously grown up on the Norfolk and Western and those who had come from the Southern Railway."

That sharing of responsibility was implemented down the line, notes Gelmini: "The two older railroads shared equally in the hierarchy of the new. Bob Claytor was the CEO and he had come out of the Norfolk and Western. But as we tiered down the hierarchy, people were chosen to make sure there was an equal blend of Southern and Norfolk and Western people as vice presidents, equally as assistant vice presidents and on down the line—directors and managers too. In fact they probably had more managers at that time and for the first several years after the merger date than they needed, but the design decision was driven by the idea of putting these two organizations together to see what synergies would occur."

It was perhaps that careful planning that helped save the company when, five years after the merger, a fairly attractive early retirement package was offered and some thirteen hundred managers left at once:

> When it was decided to offer this "early-out package," management thought that maybe somewhere between 300 and maybe as many as 400 people would decide to retire early. Actually 1,301 people said yes, which stripped the railroad virtually overnight of a tremendous wealth of experience and knowledge. These were people who had anywhere from twenty to thirty or thirty-five years with the railroad and they were gone. They just walked out the door, and they didn't write down what they knew. They didn't leave a book of memoirs for the next person.
>
> All of a sudden a number of people were promoted in the organization—maybe by the old railroad standards a little prematurely, but nonetheless there came a wave of people overnight who had assumed more responsibility and then had to act on that responsibility very quickly and sometimes without the benefit of a safety net. They found themselves in stretch assignments.

Such an unexpected upheaval could overturn a company. Again, by controlling the resulting intensity, Norfolk Southern was able to keep on track and move forward. The company's ongoing success more than ten years after that incident attests to the effectiveness of its corrective measures.

Using Targeted Innovation. You recall from Chapter Four that Targeted Innovation is a way to focus a problem to come up with more effective solutions. At the Center for Creative Leadership we worked with Norfolk Southern a great deal during the merger to help employees use Targeted Innovation to resolve a number of problems associated with that major coupling. As Gelmini remembers,

> It was a five-day creative-problem-solving course called Innovative Problem-Solving (IPS) that was used pre- and postmerger to stimulate team building between the management teams of both railroads and to help solve merger- and railroad-related problems. The major benefit was having both management teams talking with each other.
>
> Altogether about 350 people participated in the training program, with an equal split of former Southern Railway and Norfolk and Western participants each time the course was offered. About 10 percent of the management of the combined organization attended. Then the five-day course was tiered down three or four management levels to about midlevel management.
>
> The course design required participants to bring with them their own work-related problems. The experience that had the most impact was the number of ways you could redefine the problem, trying not to place artificial boundaries on the problem. People had been working on problems for years, trying harder to come up with an answer when they were really not looking at the problem from a new light.
>
> Brainstorming became a way of life at Norfolk Southern through the IPS program. Almost twenty years later it is still our common way to approach problems. Rather than someone struggling with an issue independently, they'll almost always call

together a group of three, four, five, or six people and brainstorm. They realize the value of asking people who have some familiarity with the problem, but also people who have zero familiarity to achieve that fresh perspective or at least ask some questions that will start the group thinking in a new direction.

I was among the staff from the Center for Creative Leadership who taught IPS courses at Norfolk Southern, and I was always amazed by how much people would be intrigued by a problem that had nothing to do with their area. A track person would become excited and motivated about trying to help somebody with an accounting problem, or vice versa, or somebody with a computer problem would get a lot of help from the folks who were operating trains.

Not Losing Sight of the Mission.   The kind of excitement generated by Positive Turbulence can sometimes lead a division or a work group or even a company in a direction that may seem right because it is so fresh and new. However, when applied to the company's mission, it may not be appropriate. Here is what happened once when Norfolk Southern almost went down a different track, in Gelmini's words.

Sometime around the late seventies and early eighties we started realizing that we had a very valuable asset in the fact that we owned the right-of-way—the property—over which our tracks were laid. Really, when you think about how many trains actually operate over a given stretch of track in a twenty-four-hour period, even in our so-called high-density lines, any given segment of track is only being used a fraction of the day. So the question became how can we make more use of that right-of-way, the rails, of anything, but particularly the right-of-way.

At that time companies like MCI and Sprint were competing with AT&T for communication access. So we looked into a venture of using our right-of-way to construct a fiber-optic network and actually getting into the communications business.

Here again we were exploring what business we were really in. We had gone from being a railroad to thinking of ourselves as a transportation business and then we started thinking, well, we could transport many things besides goods, commodities, and people— like information.

We actually formed a little company within Norfolk Southern called Fibertrac. We had an office and president. That business never went anywhere and as far as I know is dead now. I am convinced it was a good idea and a powerful one, but it was going to require a pretty hefty outlay of capital to put this fiber-optic network in place.

Right at the moment we are trying to increase the capacity of our internal communication network—voice and data network— to meet our own internal needs. It could get to the point where if we have excess capacity on our internal system that we might be able to sell access to others. I think that's a ways off.

More recently Norfolk Southern examined its mission yet again, notes Gelmini: "Around the early 1990s we started to look again at who we wanted to be, and we recemented the idea that we were a transportation company. Then we formulated our current vision, which is to be the safest, most customer-focused and most successful transportation company in the world. So we have tried to focus all of our more recent efforts around transportation—common-carrier-type of transportation. Whether communication fits into that is yet to be determined."

Embracing Change

In the case of Norfolk Southern, it was a major change in the guise of the 1980 Staggers Rail Act that impressed on the company the need to embrace change. The act deregulated the nation's railroads. The effect was that several major railroads merged, achieving substantial efficiencies of operations. The railroads achieved a state of profitability they had not experienced in decades. Explains Gelmini,

The Staggers Act was one of the early issues on the horizon that made railroads realize that they were going to have to change their thinking about operating and change the way they responded to customers. Having operated in a regulated, highly structured environment for one hundred plus years, our greatest hope and wish was that if we didn't have all these regulations we would have the freedom to do what we wanted. And then all of a sudden one day with the Staggers Act we had our wish, and our greatest wish became our worst nightmare.

We had people who were not used to the flexibility that was allowed in a deregulated environment. This issue brought to our attention the need to think differently about problems, to start looking at problems as challenges, and new ways to meet customers' demands. We had a history of being somewhat rigid, fixed, and that our approach with customers was that the customer needed to adjust to our schedules.

It became known that such a position was not going to help us survive in a deregulated environment. For these reasons, plus an internal desire to be able to respond quicker, better, differently than just doing things the same way (even though we were fairly good at it), there was a desire on the part of management in all areas to develop people to become more proactive to their environment, to become more aware of customer issues and to respond to them differently instead of trying to figure out how can we fit this piece of cargo into a boxcar.

It was the beginning of our realization that we weren't just a railroad anymore; we were a transportation service provider. We started to look beyond just the gauge of the two rails and started thinking more intermodal and more customer oriented, moving their freight however we could. All those reasons brought us to look at a variety of ways of attacking these problems.

Engaging Risk. At Norfolk Southern, the idea of engaging risk started at the very top. At the first IPS training session, at the time of the merger, Harold Hall, the chief operating officer of the combined railroads, addressed the assembled group. "The only practical ideas for tomorrow's business are those which contain elements of risk and uncertainty," he said. And indeed the company follows a program of frequent risk engagement, knowing that innovation often does not result from situations that follow the safe, the tried-and-true.

Take the example of Norfolk Southern's RoadRailer. Explains Gelmini, "RoadRailer was something that we invested in with the thought that the idea would eventually pay off, which it did. It is now a profitable business. But it probably took eight years of losing money for RoadRailer to actually prove itself as a viable part of the business."

The investment of eight years and many resources to pursue the innovatively creative approach was risky. However, the company felt it worthwhile to pursue the risk, and fortunately, it paid off.

Learning from Crises.   Crises, sometimes painful and taxing, can often provide valuable lessons. Norfolk Southern was nearly stopped in its tracks a few years ago when it heard rumors that another company, not a railroad but Virginia Electric and Power Company, was working out a way to transport coal through slurry pipelines. But the story has a very positive end, as Gelmini explains:

> Coal is a big piece of our business. The idea of someone else moving a lot of coal besides the railroads was like driving a stake through our hearts. So we jumped into action on several fronts.
>
> First we conducted a widespread publicity campaign, stressing the safety record of moving coal with railroads and showing how efficient and effective that method was. We showed we could conserve energy, because we wouldn't have to tear up land to build an entirely new structure, the pipeline. Also we pointed out how moving coal through the pipeline required a tremendous amount of water, and there was no real way to capture it at the end and recycle it, so this involved more waste.

Then we got busy seeing how we could improve our service. We took a hard look at the cars. Up to then we used conventional hoppers that had to be unloaded by hand or by a trapdoor at the bottom. Could we build something better? And that's how we came up with coal cars that are really gondolas with rotary dumpers. They had larger capacities, and they were built out of composite materials, so they were lighter, which meant they could carry a heavier payload and be more fuel efficient.

And we looked for ways to provide better service and decrease costs. With the cooperation of our unions, we started operating dedicated coal trains with two-person crews so we could save money and lower the cost to our customers. Another thing we did was offer our utility company customers very long-term contracts to lock in attractive rates. One of them is for twenty-five years, which is unheard of in our industry.

The funny thing is, the other company never did build its pipeline. But it sure made us sit up and really improve our service. With all the efficiencies we were able to put in, and the savings that produced for our customers, there was no reason for them to consider this alternative channel.

Gelmini feels that the steps that Norfolk Southern has taken to make it more creative and responsive have certainly proved effective; he also feels the company has a ways to travel before becoming the fully innovative organization it could be:

I would say that most customers would probably say that Norfolk Southern is the most innovative of the Class One railroads. It's not a really good comparison. We are not happy with that yardstick. To be the most innovative railroad is like being the fastest turtle. It's not a really good measure. We know that from constantly talking with and surveying our customers that they want us to be more inventive. We constantly need new ideas, new ways to get their products to market. We are being pushed by our customers all the time. We know that we can do better. We may score high for a railroad, but that's not good enough. It's a constant challenge.

Gelmini sounds more than a bit like one of Norfolk Southern's early presidents, Bill Brosnan, who believed in stretching employees to the limit in their search for new ways to do things. This abiding search for renewal has helped the company become a leader in its field and an inspiration to companies outside its industry.

Creating the Very Best at Hallmark

In 1910, at the age of eighteen, J. C. Hall, the founder of Hallmark, arrived at the train station in Kansas City, Missouri, with two shoe boxes filled with picture postcards and a desire to expand his wholesaling business. Today Hallmark is a worldwide company that generates $3.7 billion in sales annually, derived not only from greeting cards but television movies and Crayola® Crayons.

The world's largest creative staff—more than 740 artists, designers, writers, editors, and photographers—generates more than fifteen thousand original designs for cards and related products yearly and, through Hallmark Entertainment, is the largest supplier of network movies and miniseries in the world. The company manages an active inventory of about forty thousand stock numbers and serves about forty-seven thousand retail outlets.

A communications company, Hallmark is "in the business of creativity," so it is not surprising that it does everything possible to foster creativity. "Because we have to produce tens of thousands of ideas annually, we need all kinds of organizational and individual mechanisms to stay fresh and renew ourselves," says David Welty, director of new product development for Hallmark Cards. From broadening the knowledge and experiences of its employees, to drawing from the periphery, to offering sabbaticals and retreats, Hallmark has adopted many measures that lead toward sustainable renewal.

Broadening Knowledge and Experiences

Creativity does not usually thrive in a vacuum; instead it needs new and changing stimuli to keep artists seeing and thinking and ultimately producing in new ways. Toward this end, Hallmark encourages its employees to attend conferences outside their normal field, offers opportunities for travel to foreign countries, and moves employees to different areas of the company.

Attending Conferences Outside the Field. Novel ideas often arise in purely serendipitous ways—seeing something in one field and getting an idea for how to apply it to another. You need only recall Kettering's fortuitous window shopping at Tiffany to see how this may happen. As we know, one of the ways companies can increase the opportunities for such serendipitous occurrences is by providing ample opportunities for employees to attend conferences somewhat beyond their field of usual focus.

Generally a dozen employees from four different divisions at Hallmark and some senior staff attend the annual TED (Technology Entertainment Design) conference. At the end of each day the Hallmark attendees gather to share their ideas, insights, and learning from the smorgasbord of stimulating presentations in which they participated. What emerges from these gatherings is as many unique and creative responses to the same presenter and as many resulting insights as there are participants, with no perspective being considered right or wrong.

In addition to provoking intriguing discussions, this conference catalyzes fresh thinking that led an employee, for example, to come up with the solution to a gift product idea that involved glass cubes. The problem was that the company could not find glass cubes that were clear and cost-effective. But after seeing a performer from the Cirque du Soleil and Big Apple Circus juggle with acrylic balls, the employee came up with the idea to use the cheaper acrylic balls but with a small flat surface on the bottom to keep the ball from rolling.

Some other leading-edge conferences that Hallmark employees attend include the American Institute of Graphic Arts Design Conference, International Design Conference, Macromedia, MacWorld Expo, Seybold Seminars, Siggraph, Aspen Writers' Conference, and Book Expo America. They go so they can learn about the latest thinking in technology and consider its application to Hallmark. If the new technology has potential but has not yet been applied to Hallmark's related businesses, the staff creates ways to do so.

Traveling to Foreign Countries. Hallmark artists and writers are sent outside the organization to attend art openings around the world or to soak up atmosphere and inspiration from museums. Hallmark refers to this as *creative travel*. By immersing themselves in the work of one artist seen over time, by observing how a number of artists respond to a particular theme, by seeing how artists from different periods have interpreted the circumstances of their period and place, Hallmark artists enjoy a marvelous opportunity to understand better the nature of genius and the role of art. This broadening enables them to approach their own art with more understanding or from an entirely different perspective.

The only "deliverable" expected from these creative travelers is a slide show. Hallmark has absolute faith that by treating its employees to rich and stimulating environments, their imaginations will be enriched, and ultimately the company will benefit from their new insights and inspiration.

Moving Employees Around the Company. "There is nothing more renewing than changing your environment, your coworkers, your assignment and, if possible, your functional discipline," says Welty. "I strongly believe that this kind of renewal simply won't happen unless there is accountability, resources, and a philosophy that renewal is an ongoing requirement. So we rotate people, from one project team to another, from one department to another, from one skill base to another, from one country to another." The point,

Welty says, is to do "whatever it takes to assure that change is ongoing and expected."

Paying Attention to the Periphery

Much extraordinarily useful information comes to an organization
from beyond its walls (or even sometimes from deep within its
interstices). Hallmark knows this lesson well, having witnessed in
any number of situations the benefits that derive from tuning in to
the impulses from the periphery. And so the company has an active
speakers' program and a direct line to consumers.

Bringing in Outside Speakers.   Similar to Bell Laboratories, Hallmark brings in to its corporate headquarters in Kansas City each
year some fifty or more stimulating speakers. These may be "hot
minds" like Lyn Heward, vice president of creation at Cirque du
Soleil; Guy Kawasaki, an Apple fellow; and digital storyteller Dana
Atchley. Or they may be highly creative types such as Charles
Spencer Anderson, a visual artist, and Bill Niffenegger, a digital
pioneer, or innovative entrepreneurs like Stanley Marcus, founder
of the retail empire Neiman Marcus Stores.

Sometimes the talks are open to the whole company. Hallmark's internal Research University conducts ongoing guest
speaker lectures on a number of topics. A few focused on brands—
Harley Davidson, for example—and others are targeted to certain
internal divisions—a series on music appreciation for the creative
management group, for example.

Listening to Consumers.   When you consider the product lines at
Hallmark and why people purchase them, you would agree that it
has to do with the communication or emotion in the product's
content. It might deal with humankind's search for the spiritual, or
relationships among family members in all their emerging forms.
David Welty describes how Irv Hockaday, president and CEO of
Hallmark Cards, wants to develop products with emotional content

by leveraging Hallmark's intuitive understanding of consumers, its research findings, and the creative capabilities of its staff.

To listen to consumers, Hallmark has established the Consumer Advisory Board under the auspices of the new product development department. Comprising more than one hundred women who are core consumers from the Kansas City area, it meets on an as-needed basis. One idea that came from a member of this board was for Pet Love, a highly successful Hallmark greeting card and gift offer for devoted pet owners. "It's for people whose emotional bond with their pets is so special that they want cards and gifts to express these feelings on many and varied occasions," says Welty.

The function of the board, he says, is to "challenge and validate product concepts through all stages of the product development process. This Positive Turbulence often causes us to rethink our initiatives as well as take us in new directions."

Providing Periods of Renewal

While creatives in other companies tend to move from company to company quite frequently for stimulation and advancement, Hallmarkers, as they call themselves, tend to look at their employment as a career, so the corporation must replicate what would otherwise occur from moving from one company and one location to another. It does this is by offering internal sabbaticals and retreats.

Taking Internal Sabbaticals. Harold Rice, a retired officer of Hallmark and group vice president of operations, wanted to create a space where art and technology could meet. He also wanted it to be a place where employees seeking renewal and rejuvenation would have the opportunity to explore a new skill and work in a new medium and then use the center's small-scale manufacturing setup to see if they could translate the resulting concept to a real-world application. Called the Rice Innovation Center, it is a 182,000-square-foot facility adjacent to Hallmark's downtown headquarters.

Creative staff members are often given two weeks to four months to work in the studios, which support more than forty crafts, including ceramics, papermaking, fabric printing, printmaking, glasswork, and leading-edge computer graphics.

Senior designer Jan Bryan-Hunt spent a six-month sabbatical at the center, along with a writer and another designer, to study multiculturalism and how it could be incorporated into new Hallmark product concepts. Bryan-Hunt became particularly interested in the design and symbolism found in African American quilts. The result of this team's work was a new card line called Common Threads, a celebration of multiculturalism that uses writing and imagery drawn from folk customs around the world. This led to another successful card line called Symbolic Notions, which combines multicultural design influences and symbols on jewelry attached to cards.

Participating in Retreats. Throughout the year, Hallmark holds off-site meetings for the sole purpose of taking people away from the routine of the workplace, to generate ideas for future products and product lines. Often attending these meetings are external and internal presenters from within and outside the company who address some common theme or agenda item.

These meetings create an ambiance, or mind-set, about a theme for which products are to be developed. What makes these gatherings unique is that they often take place in a Victorian farmhouse at Kearney Farm, outside Kansas City. Like the Rice Innovation Center, it is also outfitted as an artists' studio and crafts center.

The goal of these gatherings is not to reward past service but rather to initiate creative renewal and, in so doing, to create new business possibilities. One writer quite accurately described Hallmark's sabbaticals and retreats as "a form of artistic cross-training—a burst of change to help keep the creative juices flowing" (Fishman, 1996).

Comments David Welty, "A supportive creative environment requires a variety of supportive mechanisms. At Hallmark, we feel that renewal activities are one of the more important of these mechanisms and that renewal is an ongoing requirement. As a result, we make available scores of internal opportunities that, because of frequency and duration, result in sustainable renewal, not just a moment of inspiration."

Committing to New Products at 3M

In 1995 almost two-thirds of 3M's growth came from products introduced that year. Two years later, 30 percent of the company's revenues came from products produced within the past four years (Dutton, 1996). These astonishingly high statistics, along with an inventory of some fifty thousand different products—everything from fire hose linings to medical supplies to sandpaper to Post-it® notes—could be achieved only by a company with a commitment to innovation at all levels.

Some seventy thousand 3M employees in more than sixty countries all over the world produce their lines of products, which are based on about thirty core technologies, from adhesives and non-woven materials to fluorochemicals and microreplication. Many of the company's products lead in their respective markets—industrial, consumer, office, health care, and many others. The result is annual sales totaling more that $15 billion. In 1997, 3M was awarded 578 U.S. patents, placing it eighth among U.S. companies.

3M keeps new product development so successful and at such a high level by developing a corporate environment supportive of innovation, promoting cross-fertilization, and paying careful attention to the periphery.

Developing a Supportive Corporate Environment

A commitment to innovation must be more than a goal of a company's senior leadership; it must be a belief borne out in practice throughout the company and in any number of different ways. At 3M this is achieved by hiring creative employees and encouraging free-ranging ideas.

Hiring Creative Employees. To assist interviewers and recruiters in identifying creative types, 3M has prepared a booklet with the appropriate questions to ask. The questionnaire came out of an internal task force that had identified 3M creative personnel and the traits and characteristics they commonly share: being inquisitive, explorative, and intuitive; having broad interests and being eager to learn and explore ideas with others; having a tendency to do first, act later, take multiple approaches to problems, and not fear making mistakes; being a self-starter, results oriented, passionate about the work, and self-confident; being committed, tenacious, and hardworking; and demonstrating resourcefulness by getting things done through working with others (3M Staffing and College Relations, 1994).

Through observing these personnel, the task force was able to formulate questions for screening and selecting recruits who would have attributes similar to those possessed by the current population of creative employees. This recruitment process offers a best-practices model for the early identification of the finest people available for interviewing and hiring.

The booklet did not stop there. It suggests how to nurture the creativity of the new recruits through, for example, pairing them with 3M mentors.

Another way that 3M finds the right employees is by recruiting them while they are still in school. Through its internships and co-op programs, 3M is able to observe and train these students for possible permanent employment. In 1994, according to the director of 3M's internship programs, 30 percent of the newly hired college graduates had interned at the company (Anfuso, 1995).

3M works closely with college professors to identify students with the characteristics they find conducive to creativity. By drawing students from some twenty-five colleges, the company is also able to benefit from a direct connection to institutes on the periphery (Pianko, 1996).

Encouraging Free-Ranging Ideas. In the 1920s, William McKnight, 3M's chairman, confirmed what many of us have determined about creativity through research: creativity is most likely to occur when people have the freedom to pursue their ideas, and this pursuit must be accompanied by the encouragement of management and the support of the corporate culture in which it operates. Admonishing his company leaders, he said, "Management that is destructively critical when mistakes are made kills initiative, and it's essential that we have many people with initiative if we're to continue to grow."

In the early 1940s McKnight sought to institutionalize the encouragement of individual effort by issuing the now-famous directive and standard against which other companies now benchmark: that all technical employees can devote 15 percent of their time to a project of their own invention or choosing. Known as McKnight's "autonomy-for-performance philosophy," it gave employees the freedom to be self-managing for 15 percent of their time. Besides the ubiquitous Post-it by Art Fry, this practice also led to the development of Dick Drew's masking tape—a signature product for 3M—Lew Lehr's surgical drapes, and Roger Appledorn's microreplication technology (Coyne, 1996).

3M takes the encouragement of fresh ideas one step further with its Carlton Society, named for former CEO Richard P. Carlton. This Hall of Scientific Fame recognizes employees for coming up with a good idea and being committed to pursuing it. At 3M half-baked ideas are supported with encouragement and the resources to carry them through to realization. Risk taking is promoted, even knowing that it can lead to failure and false starts.

Carlton recognized the importance of encouraging new ideas. "Our company has indeed stumbled onto some of its new products. But you can only stumble if you are moving," he said (Loeb, 1995).

One place that employees are encouraged to move is the "white space"—that area that falls outside a business unit's directive yet may be rife with opportunities for new business.

Promoting Cross-Fertilization

We saw in earlier chapters that cross-connections and cross-fertilization can spark the kind of synergy that is required for novelty to emerge. At 3M cross-fertilization takes a number of forms, especially foreign assignments and internal linkages.

Taking Foreign Assignments. Foreign assignments today are considered to be even more important than they were in the past. A recent *Wall Street Journal* article on executive search firms noted that in 1990, 4 percent of the searches for executives put international experience as a must-have characteristic of the candidate they seek. In 1995 that percentage rose to 28 percent (Lublin, 1996).

Because 3M is a global corporation with offices in sixty countries, it offers many opportunities for foreign assignments. More than 75 percent of the top 135 senior executives at 3M have lived and worked for their company outside the United States for at least three years.

Through foreign assignments 3M employees learn how to adapt to change and to customers and markets that may differ by country or even region. The application of this learning prepares the manager for the next assignment to yet a new culture or customer base, and the learning is, of course, transferable. The fact that more than half of all sales in 1997 came from 3M's international businesses suggests the efficacy of these foreign assignments.

Providing Links Among Divisions. 3M is quite proud of being a collective of small businesses closely linked by culture and technology rather than being a centralized monolith. For nearly fifty years 3M has implemented corporationwide trade shows, internal information exchanges that encourage active sharing of ideas, processes, information, and synergy.

Because of this culture of cooperation, it is expected that employees will seek the diversity of experience present in the company. Part of each employee's job description is to share information freely within the company. These exchanges can often extend the life of one innovation into another field.

Forging Strong Ties with Customers

Clearly 3M could not come up with the number of successful new products it develops each year without paying careful attention to the periphery. 3M puts special emphasis on being attuned to its customers.

"Our customers are a critical component in creating the future," says J. Marc Adam, vice president of marketing. "Our Marketing and R&D people must develop powerful insights about our customers. They must recognize unarticulated opportunities, that when addressed, amaze our customers. This will allow us to change the basis of competition" (3M, 1995).

Through strong ties with and a sensitivity to its customers, 3M is able to identify product trends even before they take on a force all their own. Employees look for, and get to know, users on the periphery who make demands that push the envelope for product development.

One of 3M's "best practices," outlined in a document titled *Customer Inspired Innovation*, is a laboratory/end-user interface designed to ensure that researchers in the laboratories are in close contact with marketplace needs.

The 3M vision is "to be the most innovative enterprise," "the preferred supplier in the markets we serve." It sets its sights on "industry transformation and the substantial leapfrogging of competition." In striving for realization of this worthy vision, 3M has more than simply a positive view toward new product development inside research and development; it has an attitude that permeates the depth and breadth of all functions, divisions, businesses, and management. 3M is proof that innovation in the laboratory is not enough; it must reside throughout an organization, becoming a tradition, a corporate character trait, a company's self-image. From Chairman McKnight up to the present, that has been the case.

Seeing Corporationwide Success as a Predictable Outcome

Before I began writing this chapter, I decided to do an on-line search for the words *creativity* and *innovation*. Because Positive Turbulence engenders creativity and creativity leads to innovation, I wanted to see how many times these words came up in business journal articles on Norfolk Southern, Hallmark, and 3M.

I searched through publications ranging from *Forbes*, *Fortune*, and *Business Week* to the *Harvard Business Review* and the more scholarly and academic journals to trade journals. Looking between the years 1995 and 1998, I found the following results:

- In 101 articles on Norfolk Southern, the words appeared in 10 percent of the articles.
- In 109 articles on Hallmark, the words appeared in 25 percent of the articles.
- In 284 articles on 3M, the words appeared in 33 percent of the articles.

These results show that among companies such as these three, where the mechanisms of Positive Turbulence are put into practice and the tenets of it are part of the corporate culture, you will see a great deal of creativity and innovation. You will also see corporationwide success, whether it is enhanced productivity or greater employee and customer satisfaction or expanding profit margins, because success in Positive Turbulence–driven companies is predictable: creativity and innovation lead to sustainable renewal, and it is sustainable renewal that gives companies their competitive edge.

———

In this chapter, you have seen how three companies have successfully used Positive Turbulence to take them in directions that they otherwise might not have chosen. You have also seen that because of the resultant success these companies have experienced, they continue to put many of the mechanisms of Positive Turbulence into practice to attain ongoing, continuous renewal.

You may find many of the ideas in this book appropriate ones to be considered with regard to your own organization. You fully understand that turbulence exists and, in fact, will accelerate, and that it is also the spawning ground for renewal. Hopefully, having read the book, you also recognize that useful information can be mined from disruption, chaos, and change, and that only

through allowing that novelty to flow can creativity and innovation and ultimately renewal take place. Still, the paradoxical
thinking required to implement the process of Positive Turbulence may seem too risky and overwhelming for you to want to
pursue it further.

If the above three company examples haven't convinced you
that some risk is vital for company growth and that change, properly managed using the mechanisms of Positive Turbulence, can
prevent adverse repercussions, then perhaps the following hypothetical model will.

Let us assume, for a moment, that I am the director of development for a manufacturing company. I have read this book, with all
its novel ideas from out on the periphery, and I want to incorporate
a number of them into my company in a meaningful and productive way. I need to devise a credible systematic approach that
begins by enhancing the chances that the company would be
receptive to the new ideas so that it can then carefully and
methodically implement appropriate ideas at the right time.

I might begin this process by trying to shift the thinking of my
colleagues so that they would look outward for new ideas. That way
not only would they be more likely to accept my new ideas but they
would be encouraged to come up with their own. I would bring in
outside speakers on diverse topics to expand their thinking, build
up a library of books and periodicals from many fields and disciplines, and help find ways for employees to attend conferences—
with one conference a year being in a tangentially related field to
stimulate new ideas.

I would encourage open communication from multiple perspectives and an informal sharing of ideas among employees, and
especially across groups and department lines. I would promote the
value of creativity and innovation by holding conferences, distrib-
uting literature, and recommending that human resource staff put
creativity high up on their list of skills being sought. This way they
would hire new employees because of their creativity and reward
current employees for exhibiting it.

I would be sure that research and development did not just see their job as fighting the fires of short-term problems but also understand they are in the company for the long haul, addressing issues such as discovery and direction setting.

At each step of the way I would monitor the effect of the changes on employees. Too much turbulence coming in too fast and too strongly, you recall, has a great potential for turning negative. I might find I would need to pull back a bit, go more slowly. I would definitely seek feedback from people at all levels and at all stages to assess progress and adjust accordingly.

I might identify champions of the ideas in this book throughout the company and solicit their help in promoting them. I would be sure that the champions come from all different levels and areas of the company. I might establish a cross-functional group to help further promote the ideas and secure resources and recruit people to implement them. Or, overseeing it all as a guide, resource, and clearinghouse, I would establish a companywide awareness of Positive Turbulence that is palpable. Management would take the new ideas and information, look for ways they can be used, and feed them to those who can direct and carry them out.

Further, I might seek out ways for people to stay in touch with the state of the art in every field (through joining professional societies, taking courses, and holding conferences, for example). I would encourage cross-pollination through rotating employees into different roles and divisions. Management would be expected to constantly monitor the direction we were going in to determine if the renewal process was working and if anything needed modifying.

This simple scenario gives you an idea of how Positive Turbulence—indeed, any novel idea—can be introduced and established in an organization in such a way that short-circuiting, spinning out of control, and widespread rejection are unlikely. Mechanisms are put into place to increase receptivity to the ideas of Positive Turbulence, and safety valves are available if the turbulence starts turning negative.

What you can perhaps also see from these scenarios, and most surely from the examples in this chapter, is the potential for renewal opened up by Positive Turbulence. When Positive Turbulence is not just an interesting management concept discussed by executives but a program completely hardwired into a company's modus operandi, the opportunities for ongoing renewal are limitless. When employees extend their vistas well beyond their normal purview, when management welcomes and embraces change, and when innovation becomes the perpetual goal, then sustainable renewal is inevitable. We know from current writings that it is renewal that gives companies the competitive edge. In a look at "The World's Most Admired Companies," *Fortune* magazine (Fisher, 1997) found that these successful companies deliberately stir things up, even when everything is going well, and they use new information more effectively than their peer organizations.

To do this, we need courageous leaders—with wide open eyes and minds—to extend the range of outward observation to the periphery this side of chaos. It is here, in a place that may be characterized as unclear, cloudy, and distant, that the winds of change first appear.

This book is your nautical map for steering safely through the clouds and turbulent seas of swirling new information so that you can continually discover new islands and continents. It has given you everything you need to know to successfully implement Positive Turbulence—a sense of its verity; an approach to promoting it companywide; mechanisms for developing it among individuals, with teams, and throughout the organization; and strategies for managing it.

The beleaguered Japanese fisherman we met in the Preface to this book did not have the map, but at least he knew that he needed to face the sea and its forces, not turn from them. With the benefit of both a map and an understanding of how turbulence can positively influence creativity, innovation, and renewal, you will be prepared to prosper from the complexity found in it—and not feel that change is always as formidable as a tsunami. You will be prepared to manage change before change manages you.

Appendix A: Selected Resources

The periodicals and books listed here may be useful to you as you continue your exploration of different aspects of Positive Turbulence, whether it is innovation, renewal, or cutting-edge information on business and technology trends coming in from the periphery. Also included are related organizations (and their respective Web sites) and conferences that are valuable for generating Positive Turbulence.

Credible Fringe Business Publications

Reading outside your field, especially what I call credible fringe business periodicals, offers a good way to stay on top of changes that are happening yet may not be covered in more mainstream publications.

@Issue: The Journal of Business and Design
Corporate Design Foundation
20 Park Plaza, Suite 321
Boston, MA 02116
(617) 350-7097, (617) 451-6355 (fax)
admin@cdf.org
www.cdf.org
Free; two issues per year

Design is the only discipline that has anticipated the state of affairs that exists in the new age of chaos and complexity. This periodical should be available to employees in organizations hoping to prosper in the twenty-first century. Excellent examples of how design has an impact on business success and failure.

The Baffler
P.O. Box 378293
Chicago, IL 60637
(773) 493-0413
$20 for four issues, $36 for eight issues, $50 for four issues for libraries and institutions

This irregularly published journal of literature and cultural criticism focuses on business culture. Issues are 128 pages, and circulation is 20,000 copies.

Circuits
www.nytimes.com/circuits
Published in Thursday's edition of the *New York Times*; separate subscriptions are not available.

This is a weekly section of the *New York Times* that addresses technology and culture. Updated every Thursday, it includes coverage of all sorts of digital technology, the goal being to provide information to consumers through a mix of features, columns, and regular departments.

Fast Company
Atlantic Monthly Company
77 North Washington Street
Boston, MA 02114
(617) 973-0300, (617) 973-0373 (fax), (800) 688-1545 (subscriptions)
www.fastcompany.com
$19.75 for one year (ten issues)

This publication was founded with the assumption that there is a revolution of change in the world of business and people committed to new ways of working and living. The publisher hopes to provide through the magazine a manifesto for change and a manual for achieving it.

> *The Industry Standard*
> 315 Pacific Avenue
> San Francisco, CA 94111
> (415) 733-5400, (415) 733-5401 (fax)
> www.thestandard.com
> $49.97 for one year (forty issues)

This publication promises to be a first choice for people who are primarily interested in how the Internet can help them do business. It strives to provide timely news that may signal shifts in the tides of Internet use and opportunities. The front cover of the first issue, for example, featured an assessment of the current status of electronic shopping as a profit-making undertaking. The editors describe their mission as being to sort through quantities of information and focus on practical issues. Articles are written in some depth and leave out hype and lengthy technical analyses.

> *Interface*
> www.the-times.co.uk
> Published in Wednesday's edition of the *Times of London*; separate subscriptions are not available.

This is a weekly section of the Times Newspapers Ltd. It provides a European flavor and covers technology such as games, software, hardware, the Internet, and other IT activity in features, columns, and appointments (classifieds).

> *Leadership in Action*
> Jossey-Bass Inc., Publishers
> 350 Sansome Street
> San Francisco, CA 94104
> (888) 378-2537, (800) 605-2665 (fax)
> www.josseybass.com

and
Center for Creative Leadership
P.O. Box 26300
Greensboro, NC 27438-6300
(336) 286-4404, (336) 545-6035 (fax)
www.ccl.org
$99 for one year (six issues)

This newsletter-format publication draws on the experience of the Center for Creative Leadership, which for almost thirty years has conducted research and educational activities in partnership with hundreds of thousands of managers and executives. Its feature articles provide leaders with the center's cutting-edge thinking within practical frameworks that they can use to respond to today's complex organizational world.

Red Herring
Red Herring Communications
1550 Bryant Street, Suite 450
San Francisco, CA 94103
(415) 865-2277, (415) 865-2280 (fax), (800) 627-4931, ext. 5209
(subscriptions)
www.redherring.com
Special industry rate: $34.50 for one year (twelve issues); regular rate: $69

This publication's mission is to communicate high-level business information on technology and entertainment. It covers top private and public technology companies, venture capital trends, and public investment activities.

Strategy and Leadership
Strategic Leadership Forum
435 North Michigan Avenue, Suite 1700
Chicago, IL 60611

(312) 644-0829, (312) 644-8557 (fax), (800) 873-5995 (subscriptions)
www.slfnet.org
$115 for one year (six issues) in the United States and Canada;
$135 internationally

This is an extremely well-designed publication for the busy person who
has responsibilities in strategy development or implementation. Content is divided between broad areas, such as explanation and discussion
of chaos theory (and why one should care about it), and focused topics, such as facets for successful leadership in the post–cold war world.

> *TechCapital*
> Post-Newsweek Business Information
> 8500 Leesburg Pike, Suite 7500
> Vienna, VA 22182
> (703) 848-2800, (703) 848-2353 (fax)
> www.techcapital.com
> Published bimonthly and free upon request to high-tech business
> and financial services executives in the United States, including
> biotechnology and computer hardware and software integrators and
> financiers allied to the field; others pay $25 for one year (six issues
> and three special issues).

This publication may be your best bet if you need to know how to
market a very new gizmo or concept, plan for an independent public offering, decide whether it is better to wrestle with changing
your organization's culture, or hire new people. There are no technical articles on the newest ways to send secure e-mail, but there
are articles on the issue of bringing in a new CEO.

> *Upside*
> Upside Media, Inc.
> 731 Market Street, 2nd floor
> San Francisco, CA 94103-2005
> (415) 489-5600

ups@omeda.com
www.upside.com

An authoritative business magazine targeted at the high-tech industry, *Upside* publishes information about the business of technology and offers insights on the activities of the technology industry's players and their companies.

Wired
660 Third Street, 4th floor
San Francisco, CA 94107
(415) 276-5000, (415) 276-5100 (fax), (800) 769-4733 (subscriptions)
www.wired.com
$39.95 for one year (twelve issues)

A neon magazine in which change is constant, *Wired* advertises and discusses the latest technological tools for living and doing business. It will blast you with articles from the Internet to politics and beyond.

Books on Creativity and Innovation

Because Positive Turbulence is a process for generating creativity and innovation, and because it can thrive in an organization only if the corporate culture values and encourages creativity and innovation, I include here a number of books that discuss these topics in greater depth and from different perspectives than I cover them in this book.

Although some of the books are geared more toward trainers and researchers, they nevertheless offer valuable insights and perspective for those responsible for guiding their organizations to come up with more creative and innovative solutions. Similarly, although some books may not focus per se on creativity in the workplace, business application can readily be made. View them as a source for Positive Turbulence.

Individual Creativity

Campbell, D. P. *Take the Road to Creativity and Get Off Your Dead End*. Greensboro, N.C.: Center for Creative Leadership, 1977.
With an enthusiastic personal style, Campbell presents creativity as a rewarding part of an active life. Chapters cover the nature of creativity, characteristics of creative people, family and organizational influences on creativity, and the importance of a risk-taking spirit—all presented in an interest-holding collage of advice, description, anecdotes, puzzles, exercises, and upbeat graphics.

de Bono, E. *Serious Creativity*. New York: HarperCollins, 1992.
Internationally respected, de Bono is a highly prolific, best-selling author on creativity. He can be quite professorial at times, but in this book, he leads the reader through a personal creativity training experience using examples from his consulting work.

Diebold, J. *The Innovators: The Discoveries, Inventions, and Breakthroughs of Our Time*. New York: Dutton, 1991.
This fun and useful book is a collection of true stories of the individuals and organizations that took new ideas from the point of discovery to the market. Diebold begins with the transistor, Federal Express, and cyclosporine (the antibiotic that made heart transplants feasible). He concludes with "tomorrowland"—a set of opportunities and possible venues for the next breakthroughs.

Grudin, R. *The Grace of Great Things: Creativity and Innovation*. Boston: Houghton Mifflin, 1990.
The author observes that everyone values creativity, but new ideas can always be seen as threatening to the balance of priorities concerning the use of scarce resources. People who have worked hard to secure a place in the balance in order to try out their creative ideas may resist new ideas that compete for those limited resources. This book is a series of essays on the creative act, the ethical accompaniments of the creative act, and some sociopolitical

aspects of innovation. They invite the reader's reflections rather than argue for how things ought to be.

Isaksen, S. G. (ed.). *Frontiers in Creativity Research: Beyond the Basics.* Buffalo, N.Y.: Bearly Limited, 1987.
This book reports the work of twenty noted writers and researchers in the field of creativity and innovation. It focuses on summarizing what is known in the field and raising new questions.

Isaksen, S. G., Murdock, M. C., Firestien, R. L., and Treffinger, D. J. (eds.). *The Emergence of a Discipline.* Norwood, N.J.: Ablex, 1993. 2 vols.
The two volumes, *Understanding and Recognizing Creativity* (Vol. 1) and *Nurturing and Developing Creativity* (Vol. 2), are the Proceedings of the Fourth International Networking Conference on Creativity and Innovation, and of the Conference on Creativity Research, both held in Buffalo, New York, in 1990. Especially valuable to researchers and teachers, the contents of these two books are of value to anyone interested in creativity and innovation. By itself, Volume 1 would serve nicely as a textbook. Coherently integrated, it is more than just a collection of articles. There is no other place where the person new to the field is going to find guidance on how to get started from Paul Torrance, Morris Stein, and Sidney Parnes, pioneers in the field of creativity—all in the same book. Volume 2 moves a step or two away from theory and presents more research data and examples of applications to education and training.

Kirton, M. J. (ed.). *Adaptors and Innovators.* New York: Routledge, 1989.
The author explains and applies his styles of creativity and problem solving. He explores such topics as the role of styles in different organizational climates, managerial competence and style, marketing and style, social structure, and the possibility of catastrophic collapse as an implication of creativity style. (I discuss Kirton's theory on adaptors and innovators in Chapter Four and Appendix B.)

MacKinnon, D. W. *In Search of Human Effectiveness: Identifying and Developing Creativity*. Buffalo, N.Y.: Creative Education Foundation, 1978.
This publication brings together MacKinnon's vast background in the nature and nurture of creativity. It is of interest to managers, teachers, parents, and all others who are concerned with the creative development of themselves and others.

May, R. *The Courage to Create*. New York: Norton, 1975.
Because society is in a state of continual change, May has written this thought-provoking book on why creativity is a must, using numerous historical and literary examples. This individual perspective reflects a little of May's mentor, Paul Tillich, who wrote *The Courage to Be*. The word *courage* in the title refers to that particular kind of courage essential for the creative act.

Runco, M. A., and Albert, R. S. *Theories of Creativity*. Thousand Oaks, Calif.: Sage, 1990.
This collection of research papers is relatively free from the arcane jargon that psychologists sometimes use when talking to each other. The chapters address the question of the roots of creativity in the individual; extend the domain to the culture in which the individual is supported or impeded in the expression of creativity (whether the area might be music, art, or athletics); and deal with the synthesis of creativity research and theory from other fields of psychology.

Simonton, D. K. *Genius, Creativity, and Leadership*. Cambridge, Mass.: Harvard University Press, 1984.
This book demonstrates how the author implemented his idea of "applying scientific research techniques to historical and biographical records in order to discover how certain creators and leaders came to exert such a big impact on history."

Stein, M. I. *Stimulating Creativity*. Vol. 1. Orlando, Fla.: Academic Press, 1974.

This book came out of an early post–World War II creativity study concerned with the psychological and social factors affecting creativity. The first volume presents procedures designed to help individuals, who can then work alone or in groups. The various procedures are written in sufficient detail so that readers will have a basis on which to proceed.

Taylor, I. A., and Getzels, J. W. (eds.). *Perspectives in Creativity.* Hawthorne, N.Y.: Aldine de Gruyter, 1975.
Someone looking for an entry point into research on creativity will find a variety of launch platforms for ideas in this book. The contributors include almost all of the original trailblazers in creativity research. Although some of the data cited are old, that does not mean they are wrong or have been subsequently superseded. This is a valuable reference book for the researcher of the creative endeavor.

Team Creativity

Firestien, R. L. *Leading on the Creative Edge: Gaining Competitive Advantage Through the Power of Creative Problem Solving.* Colorado Springs: Pinon Press, 1996.
This engaging, highly readable book is for those seeking to know and work from the longest-standing creative problem-solving model in the United States. Beginning with the work of Alex Osborn and Sid Parnes, the Buffalo-based Creative Problem Solving Model has made creativity accessible to many different people of all ages and circumstances. Almost anyone, after a few pages, will begin to see ways to make practical applications to one's organization, situation, or life.

Gronhaug, K., and Kaufmann, G. (eds.). *Innovation: A Cross-Disciplinary Perspective.* Oslo, Norway: Norwegian University Press, 1988.
This collection of twenty-one articles that span four levels (the individual, the group, the organization, and society) is a valuable

resource for academicians, researchers, program designers, and trainers. The articles are clustered in three sections: creativity and innovation; management, organization, and innovation; and knowledge, innovation, and growth.

Isaksen, S. G., Dorval, K. B., and Treffinger, D. J. *Creative Approaches to Problem Solving.* Dubuque, Iowa: Kendall Hunt, 1994. This is an expanded version of the authors' earlier book, *Creative Problem Solving* (1985). Designed for the person who needs to conduct a problem-solving group, it is assembled in a three-ring notebook for creating convenient packets of material being addressed on a particular day. The chapters provide background and important information about preparation for problem solving, carry the reader from understanding the problem to planning for action, and deal with personal use of the techniques. The book includes work sheets and support materials.

Kayser, T. A. *Mining Group Gold.* El Segundo, Calif.: Serif Publishing, 1990. Kayser, the manager of organization effectiveness for Xerox, has been on the front line in reconciling two favorite topics in the culture of the United States: the creative productivity of the individual and the indispensability of teamwork. In this book he offers clear, step-by-step instructions for setting up productive meetings and then moving on to establish collaborative teams.

Osborn, A. *Applied Imagination* (3rd rev. ed.). New York: Scribner, 1979. This is the "old testament" of the principles and procedures of creative problem solving, written by the popularizer and proponent of brainstorming, a method that was the precursor to current activity within the field of creative idea generation.

Parnes, S. J. (ed.). *Source Book for Creative Problem-Solving: A Fifty-Year Digest.* Buffalo, N.Y.: Creative Education Foundation, 1992.

An update of the 1967 Scribner version, this is a mini-encyclopedia for trainers, managers, parents, and virtually everyone else interested in creative problem solving. It offers a diverse selection of articles from half a century of work in creativity development and is divided into well-organized sections. It includes headnotes and an index.

Stein, M. I. *Stimulating Creativity*. Vol. 2. Orlando, Fla.: Academic Press, 1975.
See the main description in the previous section. This volume contains procedures for groups.

Van Gundy, A. B. *Idea Power: Techniques and Resources to Unleash the Creativity in Your Organization*. New York: AMACOM, 1992.
Van Gundy provides generally useful information on the application of research based on his own experience as a consultant. Theory- and research-based explanations discuss the why in addition to the how-to. The consultant-trainer interested in upgrading some old training units would almost certainly find this book a valuable resource.

Organizational Creativity

Amabile, T. M. *Creativity in Context*. Boulder, Colo.: Westview Press, 1996.
While researchers value this book as a splendid, comprehensive resource, managers of innovation and creative problem-solving trainers who want to look underneath the hood of the creativity-innovation machine will also find much of use here. The basic, original, and contemporary research is reviewed in an easy-to-follow format. Amabile presents pragmatic examples of applications of her own work and those of others interested in innovation in the real world. One valuable section describes her work with KEYS®, a measure of organizational influences on innovation and productivity.

Burgelman, R., and Sayles, L. *Inside Corporate Innovation: Strategy, Structure, and Managerial Skills*. New York: Macmillan, 1986.
The publisher describes this book as a study "that not only traces the complete new venture development cycle—from R&D experiments through staged approvals—but sets forth a basic conceptual model of the internal corporate venturing process."

Ford, C. M., and Gioia, D. A. (eds.). *Creative Action in Organizations: Ivory Tower Visions and Real World Voices*. Thousand Oaks, Calif.: Sage, 1995.
Although this is a textbook primarily for advanced or graduate-level students, practitioners can profit from using this book as a reference resource for information suitable for inclusion in advanced training in creativity.

Gryskiewicz, S. S. (ed.). *Discovering Creativity*. Greensboro, N.C.: Center for Creative Leadership, 1993.
This collection of forty-seven articles written by contributors from many countries provides an interesting slice of thinking about creativity in many different parts of the world. It is useful for gaining information about the differences in levels of sophistication in methods and the differences in problems (and solutions). The study of creativity did not begin in the United States, but the greater proportion of research and design of training for creativity was focused in this country. Now the rest of the world is beginning to regain preeminence. This volume gives a perspective on the export of peculiarly American ideas and some samples of programming developed elsewhere.

Gryskiewicz, S. S., and Hills, D. A. (eds.). *Readings in Innovation*. Greensboro, N.C.: Center for Creative Leadership, 1992.
This compilation of eighteen articles focus to a considerable degree on the development and nurturing of organizations that value, encourage, and support innovation. Half of the articles are written by researchers and the other half by practitioners.

Gryskiewicz, S. S., Shields, J. T., and Drath, W. H. (eds.). *Selected Readings in Creativity*. Vols. 1 and 2. Greensboro, N.C.: Center for Creative Leadership, 1983.

The editors selected seventeen papers, among them Don MacKinnon's article on designing an assessment center for creative leaders of the future and Mike Malone's discussion of the Army Futures Group (which gave the world the HumVee and the Internet, among other contributions).

Kuczmarski, T. D. *Innovation: Leadership Strategies for the Competitive Edge*. Chicago: American Marketing Association and NTC Business Books, 1996.

This is a practical book for people in the highest levels of management who want to learn about innovation but do not necessarily want to wade through a lot of theory or training exercise material. The author provides a platform that will help CEOs to articulate goals for innovation and the development of the infrastructure for a climate supportive of innovative efforts. Although not quite a step-by-step manual, it offers a clear outline of steps to be taken, and in what order, to help the organization sustain its movement toward innovativeness.

Kuhn, R. L. (ed.). *Handbook for Creative and Innovative Managers*. New York: McGraw-Hill, 1988.

This large book, comprising seventy chapters and more than 650 pages, is intended for managers. It provides ideas, conceptualizations, and applications (not abstract theory or simplistic how-to's). There are not many ideas out there that are not in this volume.

Nayak, P. R., and Ketteringham, J. M. *Breakthroughs*. New York: Rawson Associates, 1986.

This book contains dramatic stories of twelve breakthroughs, from VCRs to Federal Express. These are not so much the accounts of the odd but irrepressible inventors, but rather stories of the people and the organizations in which the innovations took place. It is similar to Diebold's *The Innovators* (1991; see the "Individual Creativity" section). The authors abstract some interesting lessons from the chaos and turmoil that accompanied most of these breakthroughs.

Ray, M., and Myers, R. *Creativity in Business*. New York: Doubleday, 1986.
Michael Ray is professor of marketing and communication at Stanford's Graduate School of Business; Rochelle Myers is founder of the Myers Institute for Creative Studies in San Francisco. This book grew out of a famous course the authors designed and delivered to business school students. Unlike other books with similar subject matter, this one includes generous segments from presentations that an impressive list of more than seventy speakers gave to the class. Among those brought into the course were Will Ackerman, founder and chair of Windham Hill Records; Steve Jobs of Apple and Next computers; Sandra Kurtzig, founder and chair of ASK Computer Systems; and Charles Schwab, founder and CEO of Charles Schwab and Company. Excerpts from their talks are used to illustrate the authors' points.

Rickards, T. *Stimulating Innovation*. London: Frances Pinter, 1985.
Rickards was ahead of many of his academic colleagues in making explicit the ways in which innovation in an organization is a systemwide undertaking. He has done a thorough job in connecting many of the practices subsequently recommended in how-to books to the research foundations from which they sprang.

Robinson, A. G., and Stern S. *Corporate Creativity: How Innovation and Improvement Actually Happen*. San Francisco: Berrett-Koehler, 1997.
The authors open with their observation that many solid improvements and occasionally spectacular innovations begin with something that was unexpected. The creative organization is one that recognizes and capitalizes on these unexpected events, while lesser organizations ignore them or regard them as an annoyance. In most

of the many examples, it was a single employee who detected the anomaly. Out of pure curiosity, this individual investigated it and discovered the opportunity. Much of the book is devoted to examining ways that organizations have succeeded in tapping and encouraging the creativity of the individual to benefit the organization. The ideas are accessible and practical.

Tanner, D. *Total Creativity in Business and Industry: A Roadmap to Building a More Innovative Organization*. New York: Advanced Practical Thinking Training, 1997.
In 1990 Tanner founded the DuPont Center for Creativity and Innovation after a successful career in R&D at DuPont. In this book, he captures the major insights he reached as a scientist equally balanced between theory and practice (Tanner holds thirty-three patents). He crisply summarizes theory and gives fifty-eight practical examples and five mini-case examples from DuPont's product and process innovations, beginning with Kevlar. Tanner persuasively lays out the case that the principles of innovation are real and a powerful tonic for an organization's economic health.

Tushman, M. L., and O'Reilly, C. A. III. *Winning Through Innovation*. Boston: Harvard Business School Press, 1997.
This is an easy book to read even for newcomers to the innovation literature. It provides a clear explanation of incremental versus revolutionary innovation and some descriptions of how to think about becoming an "ambidextrous organization"—one that promotes both gradual and breakthrough innovation. There are excellent contemporary examples of the two types of innovation and of how companies have been able to change to meet the challenges of being ambidextrous.

Walton, R. E. *Innovating to Compete*. San Francisco: Jossey-Bass, 1987.
The entry point in this book is a study (that the author helped direct) of the difficulties the United States was having in adopting

proven innovations in the shipping industry. Norway, Holland, and Japan were ahead in terms of success, while Denmark and the United States were wallowing in the backwash. Walton offers a macro, top-down analysis of why the United States was so inflexible and what to do about it. It is probably useful for a high-level manager or someone who needs an organization-wide overview of implementing innovation.

Books on Organizational Renewal

The ultimate goal of Positive Turbulence in an organization is to ensure that renewal is ongoing and continuous. The following books explore in greater depth and from different perspectives the concept of organizational renewal.

Adams, J. D. (ed.). *Transforming Work*. Alexandria, Va.: Miles River Press, 1984.
This collection of articles written in the area of organizational transformation puts creativity and creative leadership in the organizational context. It offers informative material for people interested in creativity and leadership at the macro level.

Cleveland, H. *Birth of a New World: An Open Moment for International Leadership*. San Francisco: Jossey-Bass, 1993.
Cleveland, a former ambassador to the North Atlantic Treaty Organization and president of the World Academy of Art and Science, proposes that the collapse of the Soviet sphere of influence and the theory of Marxist socialism has opened a window of opportunity to escape from the old traps and cycles that formerly limited the parameters of possible changes in governance and business. About one-fifth of the book is an insider's analysis of what has worked and what has not. The largest portion of the book is a series of well-laid-out propositions about how to recognize and approach the big problems of tomorrow: world security, world economy, and world development. Any manager in an organization with inter-

national reach or plans to extend beyond the borders can profit from examining this very well-written book.

Davis, W. *The Innovators: The World's 200 Most Original Business Thinkers.* New York: AMACOM, 1987.
Davis, a business commentator on BBC, gives his views on innovation in an eleven-page introduction. The remainder of the book presents brief accounts of some two hundred innovators. Beginning with Agnelli (Fiat) on through to Watson (IBM), the book showcases an interesting and not entirely predictable collection of people. Bill Gates, Soichiro Honda, and Ray Kroc are included. But so are Yan Rokotov (wheeler-dealer of Russia) and Run Run Shaw (movie mogul of Hong Kong and "father" of the kung fu cult in the United States).

de Geus, A. *The Living Company: Habits for Survival in a Turbulent Business Environment.* Boston: Harvard Business School Press, 1997.
"Living companies" are those that do not exist solely to make money, but also hope to fulfill their potential and grow as communities. De Geus found that these companies are sensitive to their environment, are cohesive and have a strong sense of unity, are tolerant of unconventional thinking and experimentation, and have conservative financial policies. The author, who was with Royal Dutch/Shell for thirty-eight years, is a major contributor to the idea of the learning organization and is the originator of scenario planning.

Drucker, P. F. *Post-Capitalism Society.* New York: HarperCollins, 1993.
Drucker discusses the transition we are now experiencing from the manufacturing-distribution revolution of capitalism to the "knowledge revolution." Although most of the book deals with the contexts in which work is and will be done, the author does not ignore innovation; for example, he says that in the postcapitalist society, "Every organization will have to learn how to

innovate—and to learn that innovation can and should be organized as a systematic process."

Foster, R. N. *Innovation: The Attacker's Advantage*. New York: Summit, 1986.
This book posits a point of view drawn from observing companies that have proved to be successful at repeatedly reinventing themselves. A sample of chapter titles illustrates part of Foster's point of view: "Why Leaders Become Losers," "How Leaders Become Losers," and "Leaders Who Stay Leaders."

Handy, C. *Beyond Certainty: The Changing Worlds of Organizations*. Boston: Harvard Business School Press, 1996.
Information and communication are the key capital assets of the new order. This book is a collection of short essays related to this thesis. The chapters cover such topics as "The Coming Work Culture" and "Be Good, Get Rich, But Stay Small." The author, a former oil company executive, an economist, and a professor at the London Business School, packages the key concepts of change and uncertainty very neatly and shows how people and the organizations in which they participate must learn to think differently in the coming new work order of the twenty-first century.

Kauffman, S. *At Home in the Universe: The Search for the Laws of Self-Organization and Complexity*. New York: Oxford University Press, 1995.
This book undertakes to translate the Santa Fe Institute's exploration of chaos and complexity theories from the math-physics domain to the more directly observable arena of biology and then human organization. The author makes the essential ideas accessible. This work opens doors on the new paradigm for thinking about how things work. Readers who are acquainted with systems theory will find much that resonates here. And from the standpoint of Positive Turbulence, it gives many possible ways to reframe pesky problems about an organization or about readers' views of themselves. At

the very least, the book points to the fantastic opportunities for new approaches in medicine and environmental sciences.

Negroponte, N. *Being Digital*. New York: Knopf, 1995.
The author is a professor of media technology at MIT. The book's central thesis is that while international commerce until very recently has rested principally on exchanges of products between nations, now the balance has shifted toward exchanges of information and the small commodities that enable information processing. With this comes a shift in the definition of the haves and have-nots to the information-rich and the information-poor nations, organizations, industries. And probably for the first time in history, the youth of the world are much more likely to be well ahead of the adults in understanding and applying these information technologies. Anyone who feels in danger of drifting toward premature industrial age dinosaurhood could profit from this very clear introduction to and update on the facts of today's communication technology.

Parker, M. *Creating Shared Vision*. Oslo, Norway: Norwegian Center for Leadership Development, 1990.
Karmoy Fabrikker (KF) was the largest aluminum plant of Hydro Aluminum and Europe's largest producer of aluminum. In the early 1980s KF was losing money and was a heavy polluter. Management was successful in enlisting labor in a major effort to turn things around. By 1985 KF was making money. This book is an inside account of what happened next as told by Parker, the consultant called in by the new managing director to help develop the program for self-renewing revitalization. Parker describes each step in KF's visioning process in a matter-of-fact manner. She makes a clear, convincing case for the power and usefulness of this process. Apart from providing pragmatic information about vision making, it is an interesting story of creative leadership by management.

Peters, T. *Thriving on Chaos*. New York: Knopf, 1987.
Like other writers, Peters also sees a revolution coming. According to him, we are in the first surges, and the biggest waves are just offshore. Peters adapts a prescriptive, how-to way to discuss this revolution. He organizes these prescriptions around creating customer responsiveness, pursuing innovation, empowering people, and building systems that support trust and organizational stability.

Postman, N. *Technopoly: The Surrender of Culture to Technology*. New York: Vintage Books, 1993.
This is a good resource on alternative points of view to bring into a visioning exercise and can provide some provocative quotations for a speech on innovation, organizational climate or culture, or organizational development. One of the author's major propositions is that technological innovations produce winners and losers. The winners are those people who quickly master the operating principles of a new integrated computer and communications system, for example. The losers are those who are barely coming to grips with the most unavoidable features of the previous phone, fax, and computer systems.

Schwartz, P. *The Art of the Long View*. New York: Doubleday, 1991.
Schwartz has produced a how-to book that also provides an abundance of anecdotal information about high-pressure, high-level decision making. As a creativity and innovation tool, Schwartz's steps for visioning are not like those in other how-to books. Although decision making may be the most distinctive feature of being a human, not many of us examine the forces that drive our decisions and the manner in which we make them. Schwartz offers scenario planning as a preparatory exercise for recognizing the alternative cues that signal the emergence of a particularly long-term reality. In this way, the evolving future is not a surprise, and appropriate responses can be put in motion.

Creativity Organizations

Following are names and addresses of some organizations that focus
on creativity.

American Creativity Association
P.O. Box 2029
Wilmington, DE 19899-2029
(302) 239-7673, (302) 234-2840 (fax)
www.becreative.org

Center for Creative Leadership
One Leadership Place
P.O. Box 26300
Greensboro, NC 27438-6300
(336) 288-7210, (336) 288-3999 (fax)
www.ccl.org

Creative Education Foundation
1050 Union Road, #4
Buffalo, NY 14224
(716) 675-3181, (716) 675-3209 (fax)
www.cef-cpsi.org

Creative Leaps International
731 Sprout Brook Road
Putnam Valley, NY 20579
(914) 528-5908

Innovation Network
451 East Fifty-Eighth Avenue, #4625
Box 468
Denver, CO 80216
(303) 308-1088, (303) 295-6108 (fax)
www.thinksmart.com

Conferences

Attending conferences outside your field to bring information in from the periphery is a valuable way to increase receptivity to Positive Turbulence. Here is a selection of useful conferences.

Aspen Institute Seminar Programs
Seminars Office
Aspen Institute
1000 North Third Street
Aspen, CO 81611
(800) 525-6618, (970) 544-7983 (fax)
www.aspeninst.org

Aimed at upper-level executives who convene in groups of no more than twenty-five, Seminar Programs focus on great thinkers on such universal human topics as liberty, equality, community, efficiency, and democracy.

COMDEX
www.comdex.com

COMDEX presents information technology expositions and educational conferences with more than sixty-five worldwide events serving vendors, distributors, corporate buyers, and users.

Convergence
Innovation Network
451 East Fifty-Eighth Avenue, #4625
Box 468
Denver, CO 80216
(303) 308-1088, (303) 295-6108 (fax)
staff@thinksmart.com
www.thinksmart.com/conferences.html

Offering inspiration, personal networking, and hands-on methods and techniques, the Innovation Network's workshops and annual conferences are gathering places for all those interested in the innovation process.

Creative Problem Solving Institute
Creative Education Foundation
1050 Union Road, #4
Buffalo, NY 14224
(716) 675-3181, (716) 675-3209 (fax)
www.cef-cpsi.org

The CPSI conference is a one-of-a-kind program packed with opportunities to build skills in creative problem solving and creativity. It offers a wide range of sessions designed to teach a deliberate process to solve problems, integrate the findings of cutting-edge creativity research, apply new tools to energize, explore and expand the limits of your creativity, and discover a new way to think about problems and change.

Human Issues in Management Conference
Silver Bay Association
Silver Bay, NY 12874
(518) 543-8833, (518) 543-6733 (fax)

For more than eighty years, this conference has been an annual forum for leading-edge thought on strategic human issues that affect business leadership, employee development, and bottom-line results. A unique event, the conference is planned by an executive committee charged with ensuring the highest-quality program possible. Held at a YMCA conference center on Lake George, Silver Bay, New York, this conference has a reputation for excellence that has helped make it the longest-continuing management conference in the world.

International Strategic Leadership Forum
Strategic Leadership Forum Headquarters
(800) 873-5995
www.slfnet.org

The Strategic Leadership Forum is an international business organization of senior executives focusing on the issues of strategic management and planning. SLF's mission is to advance the understanding and practice of strategic management as the integrative force for improving personal and organizational performance and achieving global competitiveness, a major way being through its annual conference.

Spirit and Leadership Conference
Center for Creative Leadership
One Leadership Place
Greensboro, NC 27438-6300
(336) 288-7210, (336) 288-3999 (fax)
www.ccl.org

The Center for Creative Leadership held the first Spirit and Leadership Conference in Greensboro, North Carolina, on January 9–10, 1997, and since then this annual January conference brings together more than one hundred participants with various interests in the subject of spirit and leadership. An open-space design allows participants to shape and lead discussions based on their own specific and individual desires.

TechLearn
The MASIE Center
P.O. Box 397
Saratoga Springs, NY 12866
(518) 587-3522, (518) 587-3276 (fax)
emasie@masie.com
www.masie.com

The MASIE Center is an international think tank dedicated to exploring the intersection of learning and technology, focusing on such key areas as how people learn to use technology, how technology can be used to help people learn, new models for providing learning across distance and time, and new roles for training and learning professionals. It holds the TechLearn Conference every year.

TED: Technology Entertainment Design
www.ted.com

TED is substantially different from conventional conferences; it is more like a wonderful dinner party during which conversations with unknown people in unknown professions allow you to paint new paths of ideas describing both commonalities and differences. The concept for this conference was born in 1984 out of the realization that three business and professional areas of our society were codependent, all serving the development of new ways of seeing and learning and the communicating and storing of information and entertainment with clarity and interest.

Appendix B: Targeted Innovation

Brainstorming sessions in search of solutions can often be scattershot affairs: individuals, particularly the more creative ones, in their exuberance to find just the right solution, have a tendency to let loose with ideas, spraying them all over the place. Results can run the gamut from totally useless, to brilliantly implementable, to terrific—but for a different project. Managers, especially if they are under deadline pressure (and when aren't they?), often desire a process that is not so random and chaotic yet still offers the kind of creative freedom that will lead to innovative solutions. Such a process is immensely useful in a turbulence-driven organization.

At the Center for Creative Leadership I developed a model for idea generation that helps managers enable their groups to be more efficient and more effective at thinking creatively. Called Targeted Innovation, or TI, it teaches group idea generation skills in a unique way. What distinguishes it from other methods of idea generation is its highly focused nature: managers determine ahead of time what kind of solution is required for the problem at hand. By concentrating a large amount of energy and attention on a specific target, they can then ensure that the solution that evolves is precisely what is needed, rather than a good idea that may or may not have anything to do with the problem of the moment.

TI has great appeal because it treats the creative process as something that is controllable and predictable, not random or unmanageable. It is based on the assumption that there is no one best problem-solving style and that different circumstances demand different styles. Successful problem resolution then involves altering the

177

problem-solving process to fit the problem at hand. To draw on a navigational analogy, you have a choice about the routes you can take from the starting point to where you want to end up, and your routes should be chosen in consideration of your destination.

To help determine the most appropriate approach (route), you need to look at two archetypal problem-solving styles—adaptive and innovative—that differ from one another in the way the problem solver defines the problem. To use Targeted Innovation, you need first to understand the two different styles while recognizing that most situations call for a style that falls somewhere along the continuum between the two. Then you need to understand how to choose and apply the appropriate problem-solving style and technique.

Understanding the Basic Problem-Solving Styles

The two styles were identified by Michael Kirton (1976, 1980, 1981), who observed that people have a preference for problem-solving style. Some, he found, accept the problem definition and constantly want to improve or do better while never going outside the problem definition. This he called an *adaptive* style of problem definition, and it is the more orthodox of the two. Returning to the navigational analogy, think of taking the adaptive approach as being like traveling on an interstate highway: you know the roads are well traveled, quick and direct, unlikely to cause complications, but also somewhat more known.

The other approach is more like taking a two-lane road: it is sometimes more indirect, it is frequently a more intriguing way to get to your destination, you are more likely to get lost on it, you may not encounter any pleasant rest stops along the way, yet it is sometimes the only way to get to a particular (and usually difficult) location. Kirton labeled this approach the *innovative* style. People who practice it are more likely to challenge the definition put forward, go outside it, and want to do things differently.

To understand these two different styles, think of two different ways of reassembling the Rubik's Cube's multicolored parts so that each face is one color. (Rubik's Cube is a puzzle that first appeared in 1974 and consists of twenty-six little cubes in six colors along each face of the cube. The goal is to move the parts in such a way that the nine squares on each face are the same color.)

Most people, following directions, rearrange the different parts until, sometimes hours later, they have gotten one-color faces. These individuals follow the adaptor approach. The other group, practicing the innovative style, disregards the directions; they pull apart the individual pieces and reassemble them, or peel off the color decals and reposition them—getting the same results as the adaptors.

Each of us usually prefers one style to the other, but we each have the capacity and can be trained to use either. What is key is recognizing the advantages of a particular style and applying that style appropriately. Generally a balanced approach in which one can use both adaptive and innovative problem-defining styles leads to a sounder solution and one with greater flexibility. For example, following the innovative style would cause us perpetually and agonizingly to reinvent the wheel, leaving us with no time to get around to the automobile. On the other hand, if we accept that the wheel is what it is and that it is not to be reexamined, we would be left riding around on wheels of redwood and pine. But by using both styles, we are indeed more inclined to come up with the automobile.

If you think of the differences between the two styles as being two ends of a continuum, then there is a range of different approaches. We saw this very clearly when we were developing our model for TI and posed a problem, getting back responses that fell into four categories of creativity between the two points, each reflecting a different degree of liberty that problem solvers took with the problem definition. The problem we posed was this: "The tea industry has a spare capacity for producing tea bags. What else can be packed in a tea bag?"

Category One represented the most adaptive mode. Solutions directly answered the question, "What else can be put in the package?" The answers tended to be a food or beverage—coffee, fruit drinks, sugar, spices—and the bag continued to function as a disperser.

Category Two was slightly less adaptive and slightly more innovative in style. Solutions involved a new use for the package—it was not so directly related to food—but the package remained essentially unchanged in shape and size. Some responses included putting shoe polish in the bag and using the bag as an applicator, filling the bags with sand and using them as weights in curtains, using the bags as protective cases for jewels and gems, and filling the bags with small amounts of concrete or plaster and using them as patches to fill in holes in plaster surfaces.

Category Three leaned toward the innovative end of the continuum. Solutions involved a structural change in the package, such as modifying its shape or size, but the bag was still used as a vessel or container. Solutions included changing the shape and size of the bag to that of a shoe and putting a shoe pad inside it, turning the bags into full-sized pillow cases, filling the bags with fiberglass insulation, and filling the bags with beans and turning them into beanbag chairs.

Category Four included the most innovative ideas. The solutions reflected problem definitions that had little to do with what else can be packed in a tea bag. In fact, they frequently specified not putting anything in the bag at all and using the paper material for something else altogether—curtains, parachutes, or clothing. Another innovative response addressed the issue of spare capacity by recommending getting rid of some of the tea bag stuffing machines and thereby reducing the extra capacity.

Recognizing the range of pathways on the road to problem solving is the first step in using TI. The next is to know how to use each approach so the most efficacious solution results.

Using the Appropriate Style

Most problems come with their own set of circumstances and constraints. If you were the actual tea bag manufacturer, you might instruct your research and development group that the new uses for the bags must be designed and produced within two years at a cost of $1 million. Further, you might specify that because your company has been losing money consistently, the solution needs to address the cash drain on a permanent basis. Each of these circumstances and conditions can affect your decision as to which problem-solving style you apply.

Following are some questions to ask in helping to determine whether a more adaptive or a more innovative style of creativity is the more suitable one:

- What can you afford to spend? The more time and money that you have, the freer you are to try something in the innovative style. But because the innovative style is less tested and less polished, it is often less efficient in the short run. So if you are on a tight schedule and budget, an adaptive approach might be better. However, if you have very limited resources and it is clear that the old ways of doing things will not work, you may have no other recourse than to try an innovative solution and hope that it will be quicker or cheaper.

- What can you afford to lose? The innovative style of creativity is riskier than the adaptive style. On the one hand, if you have some sort of safety net in case your solution should fall through, then you may decide it is worth risking money, time, and even credibility with an innovative approach. On the other hand, you may decide that you will lose everything if you do *not* do something more innovative. If, for example, your tea bag company sits on a plot of land you could divide and sell should your beanbag casing scheme fall through, then you can risk undertaking this creative solution. If your company is on the brink of bankruptcy, with no safety net, you might decide to opt for enlarging the bags and turning them into pillowcases, a sort of last-ditch effort.

- How often have you gotten this fixed before "once and for all"? If the problem continues to recur, it may be that the Band-aid solutions you have come up with have been the answers to the wrong problems. A willingness to try a different, innovative approach to the problem may be needed. If filling the bags with coffee or sugar still leaves you with extra capacity, you might consider abandoning the bag idea altogether and using the paper for parachutes.

- Who is going to have to like your solutions? You should consider the character and demeanor of bosses, clients, and solution implementers and choose a mode that is most likely to generate approval and cooperation. When it is important to stay on the side of credibility, an adaptive approach is advised. When the task is to do something really different, an innovative approach is helpful.

- What stage of problem solving are you at? Early in the project phase is the time to be open to innovative exploration, looking at all the different ways a project can be done. It is, however, bad form to decide after many plans have been drawn and construction started that there is a better solution. At this point the adaptive approach is needed to reach closure.

- How bad is the problem? Interestingly, this factor tends to polarize the choice of mode; it pushes people toward the extreme in either the adaptive or the innovative direction. Some say that when the ship is sinking, they will try anything to survive—innovative creativity (doing things differently) at all costs. Others say that when their back is to the wall, they will dearly hold on to what they know best—adaptive creativity (doing things better).

- How well are things going? When things are going well, there is little need for dramatic change. Change for the sake of change is foolhardy. You should beware of excess comfort, however, lest success with adaptiveness lull you into such complacency that you lose out to the innovative ideas of your competitors.

You can use these considerations as a checklist to help you decide which mode of creativity you will apply. Although each factor may have an impact (and admittedly sometimes a conflicting impact) on the style of problem solving that you choose, ultimately it is your judgment as to which factor is most important that will help you determine which approach applied to each circumstance is likely to result in the overall most suitable solution.

There is no simple, automatic formula. But by considering factors like these, you can see the sort of contingencies that are important as you assess the situation and determine which mode of creativity to apply. Once this assessment has been made and the desired style specified, the next step in using TI is to decide which problem-solving technique you will use.

Using the Appropriate Technique

Three different problem-solving techniques that we use in both individual and group settings—brainstorming, brainwriting, and excursion—differ in their ability to generate innovative or adaptive solutions. Knowing when and under what situations to use each one is key to effective idea generation.

Each of the techniques has different strengths and weaknesses. Based on a knowledge of these, a problem solver can choose a strategy that will produce the results that he or she wants. A fundamental consideration in the choice of problem-solving technique (brainstorming, brainwriting, or excursion) is the mode of creativity (adaptive or innovative) judged to be appropriate to the situation. Each of the techniques tends to produce different modes of solutions.

The key, of course, is an accurate diagnosis of the seven situational factors. Such a diagnosis is easier to suggest, though, than to accomplish. Experience and practice help. But as you progress, you can begin to make creativity work as you want it to—under your control. You can begin to predict the nature of the solution you will reach using the various idea-generating techniques.

Brainstorming

Most people are familiar with this verbal idea-generating method. However, many think that brainstorming means the same thing as "free-for-all." It does not. There are rules to brainstorming, including these:

- Generate a large number of ideas.
- Freewheel with any idea.
- Suspend any judgment of any idea until the later idea evaluation state.
- Build on each other's ideas.

Brainstorming results in a higher percentage of solutions that fall within Categories Two and Three—a mixture of moderately adaptive and moderately innovative ideas. Because brainstorming sessions are frequently punctuated with humor, the humor tends to free the group to break rules—rules that often unduly inhibit a group. Brainstorming participants then feel free to pursue more tangential modes of problem definition.

Brainwriting

This is an idea-generating process in which the problem solvers write down several ideas on different pieces of paper and then regularly exchange the pieces of paper. The rules of brainstorming also apply to brainwriting.

Brainwriting produces a higher percentage of adaptive responses (Category One). Because spontaneous group interaction is difficult in this nonspeaking technique, there is less of a tendency for the group to spur itself on to ideas outside the problem definition that it was given. Although brainwriters share ideas, this problem-solving technique is not as free-form and fun as the others. Being limited to the written medium, participants feel somewhat restricted and less inclined to express an idea. Brainwriting therefore generates a more restrained style of creativity.

Excursion

An excursion session is usually undertaken after people have been working on a problem using more traditional approaches such as brainwriting and brainstorming. Problem solvers are told to put the problem aside and go through a word association exercise. A word that has visual appeal (it is colorful, or it is a verb that is easy to visualize) is then chosen, and participants envision images that this word suggests to them.

Next, the problem solvers are encouraged to make connections between words they came up with in their "excursion" and the original problem. A group led by Bill Parker of the New Directions Group of Norwalk, Connecticut, for example, was trying to come up with a new design for mining equipment that would dig ore and load it onto a conveyor belt. The group visualized pictures suggested by the word *feed*. An entomologist in the group described the way a praying mantis eats, clutching its food between its forelegs and then thrusting it into its mouth. The new piece of equipment that resulted from this image is a large tractor that has shovels on each side (like forelegs) that "feed" the ore onto a conveyor running down the middle of the machine.

The excursion technique tends to generate a high percentage of Category Four (innovative) solutions. It is little wonder that an approach that purposefully takes problem solvers so far from the original problem results in solutions that are quite distant from the original problem definition.

Choosing the Technique

If your diagnosis of the problem situation indicates that an adaptive solution is desirable, consider brainwriting as your first choice among idea-generating techniques. If you need an innovative solution, try the excursion technique. Use brainstorming for solutions in between.

Over the past twenty years, the Center for Creative Leadership has helped managers use the TI model in their own companies, and they have found it enormously effective. For a start, it is grounded in their reality, and so they can readily put it to use. When we developed TI, we wanted it to focus on productive, practical creativity, not the magical stuff. And so we used actual managers, not college sophomores, as research subjects. We had them work on a real problem that came from an actual industry, not a make-believe problem from some unlikely circumstance.

The second reason TI has found such favor is that it deals with the creative process as being manageable. In the corporate world today where so much is unpredictable and therefore uncontrollable and market share often depends on coming up with the most creatively effective solution to the problem at hand, it is a relief to managers to know that creativity is controllable. By assessing the circumstances and altering the problem-solving process accordingly, they can direct the creative process to a desired end.

References

Preface

Kirton, M. J. "Adaptors and Innovators: A Description and Measure." *Journal of Applied Psychology*, 1976, *61*, 622–629.

Osborn, A. F. *Applied Imagination* (3rd ed.). New York: Scribner, 1979.

Introduction

Bateson, M. C. *Composing a Life*. New York: NAL/Dutton, 1990.

Hock, D. "Out of Control and into Order." Speech presented to the Reinvention Revolution Conference, Washington, D.C., Apr. 20, 1998.

Chapter One

Bradenberger, A. M., and Nalebuff, B. J. "Intel Inside." *Harvard Business Review*, Nov.–Dec. 1996, p. 172.

Charan, R., and Tichy, N. *Every Business Is a Growth Business: How Your Company Can Prosper Year After Year*. New York: Times Books, 1998.

Cleveland, H. *Leadership and the Information Revolution*. Minneapolis: World Academy of Art and Science, 1997.

Emery, F. E., and Trist, E. L. "The Causal Texture of Organizational Environments." *Human Relations*, 1965, *18*, 21–32.

Hof, R. D. "The Education of Andrew Grove." *Business Week*, Jan. 16, 1995, pp. 60–62.

Levitt, T. "Marketing Myopia." *Harvard Business Review*, 1975, *53*(5), 1–12.

McDowell, E. "Business Travel." *New York Times*, Oct. 21, 1998, p. C13.

Peters, T. *Circle of Innovation: You Can't Shrink Your Way to Greatness*. New York: Knopf, 1997.

Polanyi, J. C. "When to Leave a Scientist Alone." *Globe and Mail of Toronto*, Nov. 4, 1994, p. A15.

Preston, R. *American Steel*. New York: Avon Books, 1991.

Salter, C. "This Company's Seen the Future of Customer Service." *Fast Company*, Feb.–Mar. 1998, pp. 34–36.

Teresko, J. "Managing Innovation for 150 Years." *Industry Week*, Dec. 15, 1997, pp. 101–106.

Young, J. "Digital Octopus." *Forbes*, June 17, 1996, p. 106.

Chapter Two

Amabile, T., and Conti, R. "What Downsizing Does to Creativity." *Issues & Observations*, 1995, *15*(3), 1–6.

Dru, J. M. *Disruption*. New York: Wiley, 1996.

Kettering, C. F. "Running Errands for Ideas in As 'Ket' Sees It." *General Motors Symphony of the Air* (Vol. 2, tape 16). Dayton, Ohio: Kettering Fund, 1992. Audiotape.

Kirton, M. J. "Adaptors and Innovators: A Description and Measure." *Journal of Applied Psychology*, 1976, *61*, 622–629.

Kirton, M. J. (ed.). *Adaptors and Innovation: Styles of Creativity and Problem Solving*. New York: Routledge, 1989.

LaBarre, P. "How Skandia Generates Its Future Faster." *Fast Company*, 1997, 6, 58.

Schwartz, P. *The Art of the Long View*. New York: Doubleday, 1991.

Taylor, W. C. "What Comes After Success." *Fast Company*, 1997, 6, 82–85.

Chapter Three

Bradford, B. "Jazz Improvisation and Group Creativity." In S. S. Gryskiewicz, J. T. Shields, and W. H. Drath (eds.), *Selected Readings in Creativity* (Vol. 1, pp. 125–134). Greensboro, N.C.: Center for Creative Leadership, 1983.

Coyne, P. "TED5: Technology Entertainment Design." *Communication Arts (ICMA)*, 1994, *36*(2), 126–132.

Hirshberg, J. *The Creative Priority: Driving Innovative Business in the Real World*. New York: HarperCollins, 1998.

Kasperson, C. J. "Psychology of the Scientist: XXXVII. Scientific Creativity: A Relationship with Information Channels." *Psychological Reports*, 1978, *42*, 691–694.

Marriot, M. "In the Labs, Wearable Computers Are Becoming a Reality." *New York Times*, Jul. 23, 1998, p. G7.

Mieszkowski, K. "Report for the Future: Radical Sabbaticals." *Fast Company*, Nov. 1998, pp. 48–50.

Tanner, D. *Total Creativity in Business and Industry*. Des Moines, Iowa: Advanced Practical Thinking Training, 1997.

Chapter Four

Coy, P., Billups, J., and Hansen, L. "Blue-Sky Research Comes Down to Earth." *Business Week*, Jul. 3, 1995, pp. 78–80.

Dixon, N. M. "The Hallways of Learning." *Organizational Dynamics*, 1997, *25*(4), 23–34.

Farnham, A. "How to Nurture Creative Sparks." *Fortune*, Jan. 10, 1994, pp. 94–100.

Gryskiewicz, S. *Creativity in Organizations: A Jazz Musician's Perspective*. Greensboro, N.C.: Center for Creative Leadership, 1989. Videotape.

Hirshberg, J. *The Creative Priority: Driving Innovative Business in the Real World.* New York: HarperCollins, 1998.

Johnston, S. J. "Microsoft Invests in the Millennium." *Informationweek,* June 29, 1998, pp. 68–76.

Katzenbach, J. R. *The Wisdom of Teams: Creating the High-Performance Organization.* Boston: Harvard Business School Press, 1993.

Millard, A. *Edison and the Business of Innovation.* Baltimore: Johns Hopkins University Press, 1993.

Rosenfeld, R. B. "The Development and Philosophy of the Photographic Divisions' Office of Innovation (PDOI) System." In S. S. Gryskiewicz, J. T. Shields, and W. H. Drath (eds.), *Selected Readings in Creativity* (Vol. 1, pp. 93–124). Greensboro, N.C.: Center for Creative Leadership, 1983.

Stross, R. E. "Mr. Gates Builds His Brain Trust." *Fortune,* Dec. 8, 1997, pp. 84–98.

Swiggett, R. L. "Structuring for Innovation and the Bottom Line." In S. S. Gryskiewicz and D. A. Hills (eds.), *Readings in Innovation* (pp. 171–180). Greensboro, N.C.: Center for Creative Leadership, 1992.

Wright, R. F. "Fostering Creativity and Innovation in a New-Product Research Group." In S. S. Gryskiewicz and D. A. Hills (eds.), *Readings in Innovation* (pp. 195–209). Greensboro, N.C.: Center for Creative Leadership, 1992.

Chapter Five

"Aging Boom Is at Hand." *USA Today,* Oct. 24, 1994. p. 01A.

Amabile, T. M. *Creativity in Context.* Boulder, Colo.: Westview Press, 1996.

Asinof, L. "Offbeat Talks Part of Routine at Bell Labs." *Wall Street Journal,* Nov. 16, 1982, p. 35.

Bivins, R. "Active Adult Communities Don't Trust Anyone Under 55." *Miami Herald,* Mar. 8, 1998, p. 7H.

Bryant, A. "Perfect Match, But Will It Mesh?" *New York Times,* Jan. 14, 1997, p. D1.

Cleveland, H. *Birth of a New World.* San Francisco: Jossey-Bass, 1993.

de Geus, A. *The Living Company: Habits for Survival in a Turbulent Business Environment.* Boston: Harvard Business School Press, 1997.

Flynn, G. "Xers vs. Boomers: Teamwork or Trouble?" *Personnel Journal,* Nov. 1996, pp. 86–89.

Gryskiewicz, S. *Creativity in Organizations: A Jazz Musician's Perspective.* Greensboro, N.C.: Center for Creative Leadership, 1989. Videotape.

Hamel, G., and Prahalad, C. K. "Corporate Imagination and Expeditionary Marketing." *Harvard Business Review,* Jul.–Aug. 1991, pp. 81–92.

Kirsner, S. "Designed for Innovation." *Fast Company,* Nov. 1998, pp. 54–56.

Leonard, D., and Rayport, J. F. "Spark Innovation Through Empathic Design." *Harvard Business Review,* Nov.–Dec. 1997, pp. 103–113.

Levitt, T. "Marketing Myopia." *Harvard Business Review,* 1975, 53(5), 1–12.

Losyk, B. "Generation X: What They Think and What They Plan to Do." *Futurist,* Mar.–Apr. 1997, pp. 39–44.

Petzinger, T., Jr. "The Front Lines." *Wall Street Journal,* Feb. 20, 1998, p. B1.

Phillips Petroleum. "Context." [Video.] Wilkes-Barre, Pa.: Karol Media, 1984.

Schwartz, P. *The Art of the Long View*. New York: Doubleday, 1991.
Stross, R. E. "Mr. Gates Builds His Brain Trust." *Fortune*, Dec. 8, 1997, pp. 84–98.
"Unjammed: Digital Audio." *Economist*, May 23, 1998, p. 74.

Chapter Six

Anfuso, D. "3M's Staffing Strategy Promotes Productivity and Pride." *Personnel Journal*, Feb. 1995, pp. 28–34.
Coyne, W. E. "Building a Tradition of Innovation." Fifth UK Innovation Lecture, Department of Trade and Industry Innovation Unit, London, Mar. 5, 1996.
Dutton, G. "Enhancing Creativity." *Management Review*, 1996, 85(11), 44–46.
Fisher, A. "The World's Most Admired Companies." *Fortune*, Oct. 27, 1997, pp. 220–240.
Fishman, C. "At Hallmark, Sabbaticals Are Serious Business." *Fast Company*, Oct.–Nov. 1996, pp. 44–46.
Levitt, T. "Marketing Myopia." *Harvard Business Review*, 1975, 53(5), 1–12.
Loeb, M. "Ten Commandments for Managing Creative People." *Fortune*, Jan. 16, 1995, pp. 135–136.
Lublin, J. S. "An Overseas Stint Can Be a Ticket to the Top." *Wall Street Journal*, Jan. 29, 1996, p. B1.
Pianko, D. "Power Internships." *Management Review*, Dec. 1996, pp. 31–33.
3M. "Customer Inspired Innovation: Your Invitation to Create the Future." Summary conclusions, Thought Leader Panel Workshop on Customer Inspired Innovation, Feb. 14–15, 1995.
3M Staffing and College Relations. *Hiring Innovators*. St. Paul, Minn.: 3M Staffing and College Relations, 1994.

Appendix B

Kirton, M. J. "Adaptors and Innovators: A Description and Measure." *Journal of Applied Psychology*, 1976, 61, 622–629.
Kirton, M. J. "Adaptors and Innovators in Organizations." *Human Relations*, 1980, 33(4), 213–224.
Kirton, M. J. "Adaption-Innovation: A Theory of Organizational Creativity." In S. S. Gryskiewicz and J. T. Shields (eds.), *Creativity Week IV: 1981 Proceedings* (pp. 90–101). Greensboro, N.C.: Center for Creative Leadership, 1981.

Suggested Readings

Drucker, P. F. *Management*. New York: HarperCollins, 1973.
Gryskiewicz, S. S. "Trial by Fire in an Industrial Setting. A Practical Evaluation of Three Creative Problem-Solving Techniques." In K. Gronhaug and G. Kaufmann (eds.), *Innovation: A Cross-Disciplinary Perspective* (pp. 205–232). New York: Oxford University Press, 1988.
Kuhn, T. S. *The Structure of Scientific Revolutions*. Chicago: University of Chicago Press, 1962.

Index

More Titles from the Center for Creative Leadership

Leadership in Action
Martin Wilcox, Editor

Keep yourself up to date on the latest research and practices impacting leadership today. *Leadership in Action* offers readers the latest insights from CCL's many ongoing research and projects, educational and expert advice on how these can best be applied in the real world. Published bimonthly, each issue of this cutting-edge journal delivers in-depth articles designed to help practicing leaders hone their existing skills and identify and develop new ones.

One-year (six issues) individual rate: $99.00
One-year (six issues) institutional rate: $125.00
Two-year individual rate: $158.00 (save 20%)
Two-year institutional rate: $200 (save 20%)

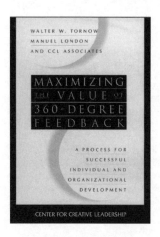

Maximizing the Value of 360-Degree Feedback
A Process for Successful Individual and Organizational Development
Walter Tornow, Manuel London, & CCL Associates, Center for Creative Leadership

In this unprecedented volume, CCL draws upon twenty-eight years of leading research and professional experience to deliver the most thorough, practical, and accessible guide to 360-degree feedback ever. Readers will discover precisely how they can use 360-degree feedback to achieve a variety of objectives such as communicating performance expectations, setting developmental goals, establishing a learning culture, and tracking the effects of organizational change. Detailed guidelines show how 360-degree feedback can be designed to maximize employee involvement, self-determination, and commitment.

Hardcover   408 pages   Item #F093 $42.95

"This wonderfully useful guide to leadership development will prove an invaluable resource to anyone interested in growing the talent of their organizations."
—Jay A. Conger, professor, USC, and author of *Learning to Lead*

The Center for Creative Leadership
Handbook of Leadership Development
Cynthia D. McCauley, Russ S. Moxley, Ellen Van Velsor, Editors

In one comprehensive volume, the Center for Creative Leadership distills its philosophy, findings, and methodologies into a practical resource that sets a new standard in the field. Filled with proven techniques and detailed instructions for designing and enabling the most effective leadership development programs possible—including six developed by CCL itself—this is the ultimate professional guide from the most prestigious organization in the field.

Hardcover   480 pages   Item #F116 $65.00

"At last, a practical, quick, direct, and easy-to-use tool that helps individuals flex their learning muscles! I'll use the Learning Tactics Inventory (LTI) in my consulting practice right away."
—Beverly Kaye, author, *Up Is Not the Only Way*

Learning Tactics Inventory
Facilitator's Guide & Participant Workbook
Maxine A. Dalton

Developed by CCL, the *Learning Tactics Inventory* (LTI) gives you everything you need to conduct a two- to four-hour workshop that introduces participants to their most frequently used learning strategies and provides them with specific suggestions for becoming more versatile learners. The *Inventory* is used by workshop participants to profile individual learning styles. The *Participant Workbook* is used to score and interpret results. The *Facilitator's Guide*, which includes a sample copy of the *Participant Workbook*, details all key workshop procedures—including setup, administration, and follow-up—and comes with reproducible overhead and handout masters. You'll need one *Inventory* and *Workbook* per participant, available at bulk discounts.

LTI Inventory within Participant Workbook paperback   48 pages
Item #G515 $12.95
LTI Facilitator's Guide [includes sample Workbook] paperback 56 pages
Item #G514 $24.95

Job Challenge Profile
Learning from Work Experience
Marian N. Ruderman, Cynthia D. McCauley, Patricia J. Ohlott

The richest opportunities for managerial learning and development come from job experiences. With the tools comprising the *Job Challenge Profile*, managers can take advantage of these opportunities. The *Instrument* has fifty questions that a manager answers about his or her job. The *Participant Workbook* contains the instrument scoring key that is used to identify the job components that are most challenging. It also provides guidelines for how to capitalize on the learning potential of these components, and offers strategies for incorporating future job assignments into development plans. The *Facilitator's Guide*, in addition to documenting the research and field-testing that underlie the *JCP*, gives detailed instructions for how it can be used as part of a training session. The *JCP*, which can also be used as a part of a program of self-study, will thus enhance learning on the job.

JCP Instrument   6 pages   Item #G108 $4.95
JCP Participant Workbook   paperback   56 pages   Item #G106 $12.95
JCP Facilitator's Guide [includes sample **Workbook**]   paperback   72 pages
Item #G107 $24.95

Available in Bookstores or Call Toll Free 1-800-956-7739
or Visit Our Web Site at www.jbp.com

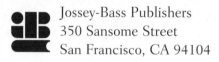

Jossey-Bass Publishers
350 Sansome Street
San Francisco, CA 94104